ACCLAIM FOR *GEEKS*

"Smart and unexpectedly moving . . . Jon Katz has delivered the most insightful and authentic study yet of the meaning of the Internet boom. He cuts directly to the humanity within, finding it in the form of two forgotten teenagers . . . Yet for all its turmoil and darkness, *Geeks* is a work of optimism. When the last page is turned, a sense of hope lingers."

—*Portland Oregonian*

"[*Geeks*] takes readers' emotions off guard, first disarming and then touching them . . . Geeks rule the Internet future, but what we have here is a love story, and a fine one."

—*Kirkus Reviews*

"A touching page-turner about social outcasts using technology to wriggle free of dead-end lives."   —*U.S. News & World Report*

"*Geeks* is a sharp cultural assessment of the way the word *geek* has been flip-flopped from a source of pain to one of pride . . . A snapshot of life that could not have existed ten years ago or ten years from now, *Geeks* resonates in what nerds like to call RL—real life."   —*The Village Voice*

"The story of these two boys pulling themselves up by their cable modems is engrossing, touching, and tragic . . . *Geeks* should be required reading for every prom queen, parent, member of Congress, or high school miscreant in this country."

—*flakmagazine.com*

"A sweet story about two teens who escape dead-end lives in Caldwell, Idaho . . . but knowing the story's ending does nothing to dull the pleasure of taking in Katz's heated discussion of Net culture, its future, and why society badly needs to reconnect with its geeks."
                                                             —*Chicago Sun-Times*

"Spellbinding."
                                                          —*St. Paul Pioneer Press*

"While [*Geeks*] has broad social implications . . . it is a highly personal tale: Katz takes us inside the lives of these two young men, shows us their sense of isolation, their complete absorption in the cyberworld . . . and their attempts to negotiate an often hostile society. He breaks through the stereotype and humanizes this outcast group of young people."
                                                            —*Publishers Weekly*

GEEKS

< < < < < < <

How Two Lost Boys Rode the
Internet out of Idaho

> > > > > > >

Jon Katz

BROADWAY BOOKS

New York

BROADWAY

A hardcover edition of this book was originally published in 2000 by Villard. It is here reprinted by arrangement with Villard.

Villard
299 Park Avenue
New York, NY 10171

Broadway Books titles may be purchased for business or promotional use or for special sales. For information, please write to: Special Markets Department, Random House, Inc., 1540 Broadway, New York, NY 10036.

BROADWAY BOOKS and its logo, a letter B bisected on the diagonal, are trademarks of Broadway Books, a division of Random House, Inc.

First Broadway Books trade paperback edition published 2001.

Visit our website at www.broadwaybooks.com

Library of Congress Cataloging-in-Publication Data
Katz, Jon.
Geeks: how two lost boys rode the Internet out of Idaho / Jon Katz.
p.   cm.
Originally published: New York : Villard, 2000.
1. Computer technicians—United States—Case studies.   2. Electronic data processing personnel—United States—Case studies.   3. Telecommunications engineers—United States—Case studies.   4. Dailey, Jesse.   5. Twilegar, Eric.
I. Title.
TK7885.54 K38   2001
338.7'61004'0973—dc21
00-045457

Designed by JoAnne Metsch

ISBN 0-7679-0699-3

05 10 9 8 7

For Rob (CmdrTaco) Malda
and Jeff (Hemos) Bates

< < < < < < < < < < < < < < < <

Geek *(noun)* [probably from English dialect *geek, geck fool,* from Low German *geck,* from Middle Low German; First appeared 1914]: *1. a person often of an intellectual bent who is disapproved of. 2. a carnival performer often billed as a wild man whose act usually includes biting the head off a live chicken or snake.*

—*Merriam-Webster Dictionary*

Computer geek *n. 1. One who eats (computer) bugs for a living. One who fulfills all the dreariest negative stereotypes about hackers: an asocial, malodorous, pasty-faced monomaniac with all the personality of a cheese grater. Cannot be used by outsiders without implied insult to all hackers; compare black-on-black vs. white-on-black usage of "nigger." A computer geek may be either a fundamentally clueless individual or a proto-hacker in larval stage. Also called turbo nerd, turbo geek. See also propeller head, clustergeeking, geek out, wannabee, terminal junkie, spod, weenie. 2. Some self-described computer geeks use this term in a positive sense and protest sense (this seems to have been a post-1990 development).*

—Eric S. Raymond,
  The New Hacker's Dictionary,
  third edition

< < < < < < < < < < < < < < < <

Geek: *A person who, for one reason or another, is considered socially unacceptable by the person speaking. A computer geek is someone who is socially inept but expert with computers. As computers become more important in the average person's life, this term becomes more often a compliment than an insult.*

—Mike McConnell,
High-Tech Dictionary

Geek: *Short for computer geek, an individual with a passion for computers, to the exclusion of other normal human interests. Depending on the context, it can be used in either a derogatory or affectionate manner. Basically, geek and nerd are synonymous.*

—Webopedia

Geek: *Encarta Encyclopedia found no matches for:* GEEK

—Microsoft Encarta Encyclopedia,
1998 edition

Geek: *A member of the new cultural elite, a pop-culture-loving, techno-centered Community of Social Discontents. Most geeks rose above a suffocatingly unimaginative educational system, where they were surrounded by obnoxious social values and hostile peers, to build the freest and most inventive culture on the planet: the Internet and World Wide Web. Now running the systems that run the world.*

Tendency toward braininess and individuality, traits that often trigger resentment, isolation, or exclusion. Identifiable by a singular obsessiveness about the things they love, both work and play, and a well-honed sense of bitter, even savage, outsider humor. Universally suspicious of authority. In this era, the Geek Ascension, a positive, even envied term. Definitions involving chicken heads no longer apply.

—Jon Katz,

Jackson Township, New York

June 1999

ACKNOWLEDGMENTS

A HOST of people supported this book.

I'm grateful to Cate Corcoran, my editor at Hotwired, to whom I brought my initial notions about geeks several years ago; she encouraged, published, and edited my first writings on the subject. And to Mike Kuniavsky, a geek pioneer. And, especially, to Louis Rossetto.

I appreciate Ann Godoff of Random House for agreeing to take on this book, though she had no idea what I was talking about. My thanks, as well, to Brian McLendon, Bruce Tracy, and Diana Frost of Villard and Random House. And to Brian DeFiore.

I'm grateful to Beverly Kees, Ken Paulson, Paul McMasters, Adam Powell, and Brian Buchanan of the Freedom Forum for supporting me at a crucial time.

I thank Jann Wenner, Bob Love, and Will Dana at *Rolling Stone* for loving this idea from the beginning, and for commissioning a story about Jesse Dailey and Eric Twilegar, thus making possible my treks to Idaho and Chicago. The wise David Malley, who helped me sort through stacks of e-mail, notes, and tapes, and Deb Goldstein also deserve my gratitude, as does Daryl Lindsey.

I'm particularly grateful to Rob Malda and Jeff Bates of Slashdot, for giving me a home on the Web and for publishing the "Hellmouth" series and the many responses to it. Ethical and gifted, they embody the very best qualities of geekhood.

Kathy Anderson and Theodore O'Neill of the University of Chicago lent an ear in a noble, if impossible, enterprise. Mike Brown of the English department at Middleton High School in Idaho reminds me that teaching can be the noblest profession.

Thanks to Flip Brophy, Ruth Coughlin, my wife, Paula Span, and my friend Jeff Goodell. John Heilemann and George and Janet Scurria were also helpful. I am grateful to Mary Robertson.

I owe a great deal to the thousands of geeks who have e-mailed me these past few years to tell me their stories, share their theories, challenge my assumptions, and offer encouragement. They are building the most exciting subculture in the world.

Most of all, I am forever in the debt of Jesse Dailey, who reached out to me via the miracle of the Internet, and of Eric Twilegar. They opened up their lives to a stranger. They spent countless hours with me face to face, on the telephone, and via e-mail and various messaging systems. They graciously, courageously, and truthfully answered my endless and very personal questions. They also made possible my first online gaming kill, on Doom. They are awesome geeks, bound for glory.

CONTENTS

> > >

INTRODUCTION:

THE GEEK ASCENSION

WHERE DOES it begin, this sense of being the Other? It can come early on, when you find yourself alone in your childhood bedroom, raising tropical fish, composing a poem, writing code, meeting friends mostly online, playing by yourself. Or in middle school, when the jocks turn on you and you pray you will get through gym class alive.

Or maybe it comes in high school, where you find yourself on the outside looking in, getting jostled in the halls, watching TV on weekends while everyone else goes to parties.

After some time, there's an accumulation of slights, hurts, realizations: You don't have a lot of friends; other kids avoid you; you're not good at sports or interested in shopping; the teachers seem to like their other students a lot more. There are few school activities you want to be part of, even if you could. The things you like aren't the same things most other people like.

The alienation is sometimes mild, sometimes savage. Sometimes it lasts a few years, sometimes a lifetime. It depends on where you live, who your parents are, whether there's a single teacher who appreciates you, whether you can cling to one or two friends, how well you can hide your brains.

Increasingly, your lifeline is technology. Computers and the amazing power they give you—to install a new operating system, to confide in like-minded allies three time zones away, to slay tormentors on the screen even if you can't do much about the ones at school—are your passion. They give you skills and competence, or distraction and escape, or direction and stature, or all of the above.

Eventually, many of the people who call themselves geeks report a coming out, not unlike coming to terms with being gay or lesbian: a moment when you realize and acknowledge who you are and who you're never going to be.

"One day in my sophomore year," a kid named Jason e-mailed me, "I was sitting in the school cafeteria watching the kids at the other tables laugh and have fun, plotting how I was going to get home early and start playing Quake. And I suddenly got it. I was a geek. I was never going to be like them. They were never going to let me in. So I came out as a geek. . . . I can't say life has been a breeze, but after that, it was okay."

Some say they get comfortable with themselves afterward; many never do. But however long it lasts, at some point somewhere, you brush against this outsiderness—among geeks, it's the one common rite of passage. A few carry the scars around with them for good. Sometimes they hurt themselves. Sometimes—rarely—they hurt other people. But if you're lucky, you move past it, perhaps to a college where Others go. You find a community, a place where you're welcome.

For the first time, you're important, vital, on the inside; a citizen of an amazing new nation. You can instantly connect with the others like you. Being smart isn't a liability; it's usually the only thing that matters.

Whether you're a programmer or Web designer or developer, an artist, help-desk geek, or tech supporter, a filmmaker or writer, you're a part of the Geek Ascension. People need you. They hire you. They can't afford to be contemptuous. Life isn't a breeze, but it sure is different. You have an open invitation to what is, at the moment, the greatest party in the world: the Internet and the World Wide Web.

THE RISE OF THE GEEKS

I CAME face to face with the Geek Ascension at an ugly suburban Chicago cable-TV studio on a bitter winter morning in 1996, toward the end of a contentious tour for my first nonfiction book.

Virtuous Reality was a collection of essays about kids, culture, violence, and morality, a loosely focused defense of screen culture—the Net, the Web, TV, movies—against the politicians, journalists, and academics banging the drums, then and now, about the looming collapse of civilization. It was a position, therefore, that had prompted weeks of media sparring with members of the so-called intelligentsia and representatives of groups that had *decency* in their titles. I was the degenerate, the anti-Christ, a champion of porn and perversion.

The tour was winding down, thankfully, when I arrived for this predawn breakfast show. There was hardly anyone in the building but the anchorman, a handful of cameramen, the control-room techs, a producer, my book-tour escort, and me. Outside, the wind was howling; my fingers, though I was gripping a cup of coffee, were numb.

Watching the monitor in the green room, I saw Brian, the anchor, launch into the by-now-familiar tease of the segment as the inevitably frenetic producer guided me through makeup, prepped me for about ninety seconds, hustled me into the studio.

"Here's an interesting point of view," I heard the anchor say cheerfully just before I walked onto the set. "A former TV producer—and a father—who says the Internet *isn't* a dangerous place for your kids!"

I was wearing out, worn down by weeks of arguing. I was sick of myself, of the blah-blah coming out of my interviewers' mouths and my own. I was even more sick of people like this Parents for Decency flak, on the phone from Washington, D.C., where spokesmen for decency all seem to be.

"Just last week, a nine-year-old girl was lured into a park by some pervert online and raped," she announced in professional alarm. "Is that the kind of thing Mr. Katz wants us to ignore?"

Brian appeared stunned. "That sounds awful," he said, suddenly less friendly. "What about that?"

"Brian," I snapped, "it seems so dumb for us to be sitting here in a TV studio—with all the junk that you people put on the air all day, from soap operas to freeway shootings—and have to actually argue that the Internet isn't a dangerous place. Kids are more likely to have planes fall on their heads than to get hurt on the Net."

Brian and I were both startled to hear the sound of applause coming from somewhere in the cavernous studio. Brian flushed, hesitated, then plowed on. Shocked, I looked around. Two cameramen were standing right on the studio floor clapping. So were a handful of techs inside the darkened control room, nodding at me, smiling and waving, giving me the thumbs-up, and yelping, "Yeah!" and "Awright!"

In a past life, I'd been executive producer of *The CBS Morning News*. I knew how CBS management—or I, for that matter—would have reacted to such an outburst. Blood would have been spilled.

In fact, Brian was livid when we went to a commercial. "The bastards, I can't believe they did that."

"Jeez," I said, still startled but pleased. "How do they get away with that? I would think they'd get fired."

"Are you kidding?" Brian muttered through gritted teeth. "We just built a new digitalized control room and automated camera system. We're still working out the bugs. How could we fire those guys? Nobody else could possibly run the damn place!"

On the way out, I stopped by the control room. Three kids were sitting at the blinking, beeping, spaceship-like console, beaming at me and high-fiving each other. They had scraggly longish hair and were wearing T-shirts—one *Star Trek*, one that said HACKERS DO WANT SEX! and one that really caught my attention: GEEK AND PROUD.

I made the rounds, shaking hands, collecting good wishes and slaps on the back like a candidate working the crowd. Nothing remotely like this had happened on any of my previous book tours. I liked it. "Hey thanks," I said. "I appreciate that. I hope you don't get in trouble."

The three of them snorted. "Hey, no sweat," one answered. "We're safe in here, man. There are a hundred pretty-boy anchors they could hire. And they change general managers every other month. But we've been here for two years. We set this control room up. The cameras, graphics, and commercial scripts are fully computerized, all digitalized. We worked up the programs that run the studio. We are the only irreplaceable people in the building. Welcome to the geek kingdom."

During the tour, I'd been filing daily *Virtuous Reality* book tour reports to Hotwired, the website I wrote for. Readers followed my travels, critiqued my press interviews, showed up at book signings, called in to chat on talk shows. So I reported my encounter with the control-room crew in a column headlined "The Rise of the Geeks." The next day, I had hundreds of e-mail messages from people all over the country, proudly claiming the name for themselves.

It was eye-opening. The definition of "geek" no longer had anything to do with biting the heads off chickens. These self-proclaimed geeks invited me to visit their offices, studios, and homes. "We run the systems that run the world," one e-mailed me from New York. "Until recently, most CEOs wouldn't have let us in the door. Now we sit next to the CEOs. We are the only people who know how the place operates, how to retrieve files, how to keep the neural systems running. We are the indispensables."

I'd been inducted, suddenly, into a previously secret society. Wherever I went—Wisconsin Public Radio, CNN, radio stations in L.A. and San Francisco—these mostly young men in T-shirts, more secure and cheerful than almost everybody around them, came up and introduced themselves, patted me on the back, offered to take me out for pizza, warned me about nasty anchors and interviewers. They were all walking billboards for *Star Wars,* various ISPs, *Beavis and Butt-Head,* diverse websites and computer games.

As I learned more, I wrote several additional Hotwired columns about geekhood, and e-mail responses poured in by the metric ton. They flowed in for months. I'm still getting them.

THEIRS IS an accidental empire. Almost no one foresaw the explosion of the Internet or its mushrooming importance. "The Internet's pace of adoption eclipses all other technologies that preceded it," a U.S. Commerce Department report declared in 1998. "Radio was in existence thirty-eight years before fifty million people tuned in; TV took thirteen years to reach that benchmark. Sixteen years after the first PC [personal computer] kit came out, fifty million people were using one. Once it was opened to the general public, the Internet crossed that line in four years." Although most Americans had never even heard the term a generation ago, the United States will have more than 133 million Net users this year, according to the *Computer Industry Almanac.*

Historians can point to other periods of astonishing technological upheaval—the Renaissance, the Industrial Revolution—but they're hard pressed to find a similar convergence of a particular subculture and an explosive economic boom. Tech

industries are growing so quickly that almost anything you publish about them is instantly dated. A finding like the American
Electronics Association's 1997 estimate that the U.S. high-tech
industry employed 4.3 million workers is inaccurate as this is
being written and will be more inaccurate when it's read.

But the sense of limitless prospects for geeks is confirmed by
the job market itself. At the beginning of 1998, the Commerce
Department reported that about 190,000 U.S. information
technology jobs were going begging at any given time, and that
close to 100,000 new ones would be created annually for the
next decade. The three fastest-growing occupations over the
next several years, the Bureau of Labor Statistics added, will
be computer scientists (who can work as theorists, researchers,
or inventors), computer engineers (who work with the hardware or software of systems design and development, including
programming or networking), and systems analysts (who solve
specific computer problems, and adapt systems to individual
and or corporate needs).

Geeks, then, are literally building the new global economy,
constructing and expanding the Internet and the World Wide
Web as well as maintaining it. They're paid well for their skills:
Starting salaries for college grads with computer degrees average
$35,000 to $40,000, says the National Association of Colleges
and Employers, but the demand is so intense that many geeks
forego or abandon college. Elite geek-incubators like Caltech,
Stanford, and MIT complain that some of their best students
abandon graduate school for lucrative positions in technology industries. Top-tier recruits not only command high salaries, but
the prospect of stock-option wealth before they're thirty.

A society that desperately needs geeks, however, does not have to like them. In fact geeks and their handiwork generate considerable wariness and mistrust. Historians of technology like Langdon Winner have written that throughout history, widespread unease about science and technology has amounted almost to a religious upheaval.

Notice the moral outrage present in so much contemporary media coverage and political criticism of technology. Critics lambaste overdoses of TV-watching, violent video games, and porn on the Net; they warn of online thieves, perverts, vandals, and hate-mongers; they call for V-chips, blocking and filtering software, elaborate ratings systems. They even want the Ten Commandments posted, like reassuring sprigs of wolfbane, in public schools.

If we are outraged and frightened by the spread of new technology, how are we supposed to feel about the new techno-elite busily making it all possible? "Why do I get this feeling that they—all of them, politicians, teachers, bosses—hate us more than ever?" e-mailed Rocket Roger in the week after the Columbine High School tragedy.

Not surprisingly, geeks can harbor a xenophobic streak of their own. Geeks often see the workplace, and the world, as split into two camps—those who get it and those who don't. The latter are usually derided as clueless "suits," irritating obstacles to efficiency and technological progress. "We make the systems that the suits screw up," is how one geek described this conflict.

The suits, in turn, view geeks as antisocial, unpredictable, and difficult, though they need them too badly to do much

xxvi <   INTRODUCTION

about it. They resent the way geeks' strong bargaining power exempts them from having to mainstream, to "grow up," the way previous generations did when they entered the work-force.

Why shouldn't they have autonomy and power? geeks respond; they can be unnervingly arrogant. Geeks know a lot of things most people don't know and can do things most people are only beginning to understand.

Until now, nerds and geeks (and their more conventional predecessors, the engineers), marginalized as unglamorous, have never had great status or influence. But the Internet is the hottest and hippest place in American culture, and the whole notion of outsiderness has been up-ended in a world where geeks are uniquely—and often solely—qualified to operate the most complex and vital systems, and where the demand for their work will greatly exceed their ability to fulfill it for years to come.

For the first time ever, it's a great time to be a geek.

DEFINING GEEKHOOD

WHAT, EXACTLY, is a geek?

After years of trying to grapple with the question, I still find it largely unanswerable. Continually meeting and corresponding with geeks has made my idea broader than the stereotype of the asocial, techno-obsessed loner.

For one thing, you can hardly be a geek all by yourself. The online world is one giant community comprised of hundreds of thousands of smaller ones, all involving connections to other people. The geekiest hangouts on the Net and Web—the open source and free software movement sites—are vast, hivelike communities of worker geeks patching together cheap and efficient new software that they distribute freely and generously to one another. That's not something loners could or would do.

In fact, the word "geek" is growing so inclusive as to be practically undefinable. I've met skinny and fat geeks, awkward and charming ones, cheerful and grumpy ones—but never a dumb one.

Still, in the narrowest sense, a contemporary geek is a computer-centered obsessive, one of the legions building the infrastructure of the Net and its related programs and systems. Geeks are at its white-hot epicenter.

Beyond them are the brainy, single-minded outsiders drawn to a wide range of creative pursuits—from raves to Japanese animation—who live beyond the contented or constrained mainstream and find passion and joy in what they do. Sometimes they feel like and call themselves geeks.

The truth is, geeks aren't like other people. They've grown up in the freest media environment ever. They talk openly about sex and politics, debate the future of technology, dump on revered leaders, challenge the existence of God, and are viscerally libertarian. They defy government, business, or any other institution to shut down their freewheeling culture.

And how could anyone? Ideas *are* free, literally and figuratively. Geeks download software, movies, and music without charge; they never pay for news or information; they swap and barter. Increasingly, they live in a digital world, one much more compelling than the one that has rejected or marginalized them. Being online has liberated them in stunning ways. Looks don't matter online. Neither does race, the number of degrees one has or doesn't have, or the cadence of speech. Ideas and personalities, presented in their purest sense, have a different dimension.

Geeks know—perhaps better than anyone—that computers aren't a substitute for human contact, for family and friends, for neighborhoods and restaurants and theaters. But cyberspace is a world, albeit a virtual one. Contact and community mean somewhat different things there, but they are real nonetheless.

THE ROOTS of the term are important. At the turn of the century, "geek" had a very particular meaning—geeks were the destitute nomads who bit the heads off chickens and rats at circuses and carnivals in exchange for food or a place to sleep.

For nearly seventy years, the term was unambiguously derisive, expanding to label freaks, oddballs, anyone distinctly nonconformist or strange.

But in the 1980s, a number of sometimes outcast or persecuted social groups in America—blacks, gays, women, nerds—began practicing language inversion as a self-defense measure. They adopted the most hateful words used against them as a badge of pride.

Rappers began singing about "niggas" and gay activists started calling themselves "queers." A motorcycle group called Dykes on Bikes roared proudly at the head of gay pride parades. Young women invoked "grrrl" power. The noxious terms became the coolest—a cultural trick that, for their targets, seemed to remove the words' painful sting.

Similarly, as hacker and writer Eric Raymond suggests, in the nineties the word "geek" evoked newer, more positive qualities.

As the Internet began to expand beyond its early cadre of hackers, some like-minded tenants in Santa Cruz, Austin, San Francisco, and Ann Arbor began dubbing their communal homes "geek houses." Formed at a time when the wide-bandwidth phone lines necessary to explore the Net were expensive and rare, these enclaves became techno-communities, sharing sometimes pirated T-1 lines and other requirements. The bright students they attracted used technology not to isolate themselves, as media stereotypes would have it, but to make connections.

The geek houses didn't last long. Faster and cheaper modems, ISDN and T-1 lines and other useful developments for data transmission became ubiquitous, spread to offices and university campuses, and made techno-communities almost instantly obsolete.

But the term kept spreading, picked up by the smart, obsessive, intensely focused people working to build the Internet and the World Wide Web—programmers, gamers, developers, and designers—and by their consumers and allies beyond. Geek chic—black-rimmed glasses, for instance—became a fashion trend. Bill Gates was a corporate geek, a category inconceivable a decade earlier, and no one was laughing. As the Web became culturally trendy, the image of its pale and asocial founders faded. Now it's amusing to see the term "geek" springing up almost everywhere—on TV shows (you know you've arrived when a network launches a primetime series called *Freaks and Geeks*), in advertising, on T-shirts and baseball caps. And appropriated by people who wouldn't have given a real geek the time of day just a few years ago.

People e-mail me all the time asking if they are geeks.

In this culture, I figure people have the right to name themselves; if you feel like a geek, you are one. But there are some clues: You are online a good part of the time. You feel a personal connection with technology, less its mechanics than its applications and consequences. You're a fan of *The Simpsons* and *The Matrix*. You saw *Phantom Menace* opening weekend despite the hype and despite Jar Jar. You are obsessive about pop culture, which is what you talk about with your friends or coworkers every Monday.

You don't like being told what to do, authority being a force you see as not generally on your side. Life began for you when you got out of high school, which, more likely than not, was a profoundly painful experience. You didn't go to the prom, or if you did, you certainly didn't feel comfortable there. Maybe your parents helped you get through, maybe a teacher or a soulmate.

Now, you zone out on your work. You solve problems and puzzles. You love to create things just for the kick of it. Even though you're indispensable to the company that's hired you, it's almost impossible to imagine yourself running it. You may have power of your own now—a family, money—yet you see yourself as one who never quite fits in. In many ways, geekdom is a state of mind, a sense of yourself in relation to the world that's not easily rewritten.

THE UR-GEEK AND HIS TRIBE

PONDERING GEEKNESS and its meaning, I made an excursion to Berkeley last year to put the question to somebody I trusted to know: Louis Rossetto, founder of *Wired* magazine.

The trip was a pilgrimage and an excuse. Louis was a geek in every sense of the word as I understood it, although not without his considerable contradictions: He lived and worked outside the mainstream, eschewed suits and "suits," was short on patience and social skills but passionate about the power of digital technology to reshape the world. I had written for Louis for five happy years, until he lost control of his magazine in a bitter financial wrangle and *Wired* was acquired by the Condé Nast Publishing Group.

I met him in the early nineties when I was media critic for *Rolling Stone* and got an unexpected e-mail: Louis was coming to New York on a business trip and invited me to dinner. There was no small talk of any sort in the message, no chat, no preamble. What he sent was a long and thoughtful invitation to write for *Wired*—a summons, really—accompanied by a wonderful screed about the Internet blasting away corrupt Eastern media institutions and replacing them with a new culture in which nothing would be the same—not words, images, businesses, or institutions.

A few years earlier, Louis had come out of nowhere—Amsterdam, in fact—to peddle his notion for a magazine about the computer culture. In Europe, he'd published a forerunner, a magazine called *Language Technology* that then became

Electric Word. Now he thought America was ripe for such a publication, an idea almost universally rejected until *Wired* eventually made its debut and hit the magazine industry like a nuke.

Our dinner, Louis proposed, would take place at a coffee shop on Eighth Avenue. This was a surprise; media moguls that I'd dined with usually preferred Orso or, if truly anxious to signal their importance, had sandwiches brought into the office. I e-mailed somebody I knew at *Wired* to ask what Louis was like.

"Well," my friend replied, "we just had our annual Election Day meeting in which Louis calls the whole staff together and urges us all not to vote, so that we won't be supporting a useless, outdated, two-party political system."

I fell in love.

When I bought some copies of the magazine, I was further mesmerized. The cover was a luminous orange; some strange purple graphic blotted out most of the text on the contents page; and an incomprehensible quote about the future was sprawled across a staggeringly expensive four-page color spread up front.

Everyone I knew in New York, including editors at *Rolling Stone, New York,* and *GQ,* jeered at *Wired.* It was ugly. It was silly. It was, well, geeky. And doomed. Computers would never grow much beyond a small group of nerds. The middle-class, whose dollars advertisers lusted for, would never embrace computers; thus nobody would ever make money with a computer magazine. Kids would never read it. Or, only kids would read it. It was incomprehensible, indulgent crap. The Net was a fringe medium, a toy, a fad. *Wired* was a brutal rebuke to the ingrown, narcissistic media culture of New York, where no story could be more important or interesting than the people who covered it.

Inside *Wired*, the stories were text-heavy and surprising, sometimes brilliant features about the wiring of the world, sometimes rambling manifestos about how the Internet would one day transform all of civilization.

The magazine violated every publishing precept and was almost immediately ragingly successful. It launched a counter-culture that elbowed the increasingly resentful rock-and-rolling baby boomers aside for good and created a parallel nation, almost entirely constructed and inhabited by the people called geeks.

Intrigued, I sat in a Greek coffee shop and watched the door for the arrival of a man who had described himself as pale, skinny, and rumpled. A half hour or so after the appointed time, a pale, skinny, and rumpled man wearing a worn black sweatshirt that said *Wired* in barely visible letters, with the hood up over his head, came in and scanned the tables. My first thought was that this was the Unabomber; he rather resembled the hooded visage on the "wanted" posters being circulated by the FBI.

Louis sat down and ordered some tea. He wasn't hungry.

He talked like a Trotskyite, all fierce idealism, taking off on amazing riffs about history and politics, but also making it clear that he wanted to make a lot of money. He imagined a *Wired* media empire that would trumpet news of the coming revolution all over the world. For some reason, he took it as a given that I was potentially a kindred spirit who just didn't get it—yet.

He wanted the old media, which he reviled and castigated

continuously, to love *Wired* and appreciate what he had done. (He was always astonished and hurt when they didn't.) He hated Wall Street; he wanted Wall Street to give him money. He had sometimes brilliant, sometimes barely fathomable visions for the future. Some of them came to pass.

A radical, even a revolutionary, it was easy to picture Louis tossing bricks outside the Bastille or running through the streets of Moscow with the Cossacks in hot pursuit. Yet he was approachable, too, at least if he found you interesting. If he didn't, he wasted no time in letting you know it.

The news about computers, he announced, wasn't about money, but ideas—how they could be manipulated, reproduced, stored, represented, combined, and connected. Computers and the Net would transform everything; nobody and no institution would remain untouched—not scientists, academics, artists, politicians, journalists, homemakers, doctors, lawyers, or schoolkids. Computing was no longer the sole province of nerds and engineers but also the new locus of creative people—poets, painters, novelists, critics. These, he said, were the geeks. It was probably the first time I remember hearing the word outside the context of freaks and carnivals, and I was momentarily startled. But it was just a word, a passing reference, and it didn't surface again for a while.

Computing had always been seen as a scientific process, Louis went on, but that was shortsighted. Networked computers were a medium, a world, a nation even—a new thing, a new method, a new process. Imagine words and images as fluid, mutable, nonlinear; all broken down into data, bits, atoms; all transmitted freely around the world to anyone with the right machine.

He pulled out several articles, some reprints of Net writings, early copies and prototypes of *Wired* and tossed them all at me. He peppered me with questions, harangued me with diatribes. I'd rarely met a magazine editor with such raw enthusiasm; the ones I knew tended to talk about marketing plans and demographics.

We talked about the Net and about Louis's idea of a civil society. We talked about Elvis and Thomas Paine. One thing you can be sure of, he told me, as he picked up the check before I had finished eating: the media I'd worked in were done, over. Newspapers were tired, stuffy, aging. Network TV was finished. The slick magazines, all of which featured the same celebrities on the same covers, were dinosaurs. None of them had anything to say to the young, to the future.

Was I coming or not? he asked abruptly.

Where? I stammered, thinking for a second that he meant San Francisco.

"Along," he said.

"Sure."

Good, he said, because otherwise, a media critic like me would soon have nothing to write about.

He tossed his backpack over his shoulder and got up. He was sorry he had to go, he said, but he had to get up early the next morning to get out to Bell Labs in New Jersey. They were doing a lot of neat stuff.

For the next few years, I had more fun than I'd ever had in my life writing for *Wired,* then for its website Hotwired as well.

In stunning contrast to the from-the-top-down world of Eastern media, where publishers and editors huddle constantly to decide what they want writers to write, Louis was a profoundly libertarian, if undisciplined, editorial genius. He overreached, alienated, and offended. But he also captured and advanced a revolutionary culture.

What happened to *Wired* was almost mythical, of course, following the inexorable march of modern American capitalism and its Darwinian laws. Louis overextended his revolution. After building the magazine, he hired platoons of brilliant geeks to develop the ambitious and expensive Hotwired. He launched British and Japanese editions of the magazine, followed by a book-publishing division and an ill-fated and short-lived TV show.

In July 1996, *Wired* offered its stock to Wall Street. The IPO failed to attract enough investors, and was withdrawn. The company that had defined the digital revolution so spectacularly was firmly rebuffed by the existing order. And the man who had helped spark the revolution was soon back on the outside—the traditional geek fate. Louis eventually lost control of everything in the *Wired* empire and retreated to the Berkeley Hills with his wife, *Wired* publisher Jane Metcalfe, where, in the next few years they had two children, Zoe and Orson.

Louis and I stayed in touch via e-mail. We never talked about the financial or legal maneuverings, but it was clear he was devastated by the loss of *Wired,* uncharacteristically depressed, in pain, uncertain about what to do next.

Condé Nast, the publisher of slick, sweet-smelling magazines like *Glamour* and *Details,* quickly purged *Wired* of the ideas, arguments, and rhetoric that had been the hallmarks of Louis and his strange band of cyber-theorists. If the new *Wired* was intelligent and professional, it also seemed bland, focused on celebrity, business, and machinery. It became the very kind of medium that Louis had always railed against. Not long afterward, Hotwired was also sold off, to the Net company Lycos.

I'd retreated back to *Rolling Stone* before *Wired*'s new editors had a chance to toss me out, which they clearly were eager to do. Louis had e-mailed me his regrets when he'd heard I'd left.

Publicly, he had vanished, at least in the media sense. He was rumored to be involved in the legal and financial maneuverings over the sale of the magazine. He had refused to say anything to the press.

I felt almost superstitious about not starting this book without his input and his blessing, however. Though he'd hardly given an interview since his retreat, he agreed to see me and e-mailed elaborate directions to his house.

Louis's aerie proved accessible only by footpath. His son, Orson, was running around with his nanny, while workmen banged and hammered at the residence, which hung above San Francisco Bay. Louis made a cup of tea, then sat down on a couch.

He looked fit, but saddened, the pain visible in his eyes. But he was warm and welcoming. When I told him about my book and asked how he defined a geek, he grew instantly animated, leaning forward and waving his hands as he always did when captivated by an idea.

My own sense of a geek, I prompted, centered around the idea of alienation. That was part of what fascinated me, not the technology, but the seemingly common experience of life outside the mainstream, life with resentment and some pain. It seemed a thread linking the residents of the burgeoning Geek Kingdom.

Louis had little time for emotional deconstruction. Alienation was part of life for him and people like him, the ticket you paid to get in, neither surprising nor, to him, particularly interesting.

Class used to be about race, gender, social standing—old ideas, he said. Geeks were involved with the new ones. "The new cultural class has no physical demands or restrictions," he said. "There are music geeks and dance geeks. Geekdom is evolving. Anybody who is obsessed with a topic and becomes completely one with it . . . whether it's computers, music, or art—geeks come into that. Geeks is sometimes about technology but mostly, it's about brains, and about being resented for being smart."

He told me a story about the first time he met Bill Atkinson, "one of the people who worked on the Macintosh with Steve Jobs back at the beginning. He engineered the interface. I met him in Amsterdam when he was going around promoting a new Apple product called Hypercard. After our interview, we went out to the center of town, where we sat at a street café and watched the amazing people go by. He'd never been to Amsterdam before.

"He was there with a colleague, another nerd. And suddenly they started talking about calling home to find out what was on *Star Trek*; the first episode of the second series was debuting that night. And it struck me: These guys don't just make technology because they're paid for it, they do it because they like it, and they like it because of how it works and because of what it makes possible. They like it because they find aspects of it really cool.

"All geeks have this magpie sensibility, right up to and including Gates," he went on, warming up now. "Jobs says 'insanely great,' and Gates says 'really neat,' and what they both really mean is that they like the ingenuity, smartness, cleverness, intelligence, just plain coolness of stuff."

Then, lapsing into the sixties' jargon that marked his own youth, he said, "Geeks are cats who dig a special kind of cool. It's the newest cool, the cool of the new—and there's nothing sleeker, shinier, and newer than the human race's latest scientific intuitions that alter the universe."

Most of the editors and publishers I knew didn't want to talk about geeks at all. Louis would talk about them forever. "Because they revel in redefining what's possible, they are inherently revolutionaries," he went on, getting excited. "They live to hallucinate new visions, to invent the next big thing, to prove the smug adherents of the status quo wrong. For the longest time, they were unappreciated, servants to bureaucrats and politicians in whatever organization they were part of, a benign cult relegated to the margins of social respectability. But in a world where the human mind is the most precious node on the planet's nervous system, pure meritocracy is not only possible and desirable, but inevitable."

A few years earlier, a vintage Louis rant like this would have been emblazoned, along with suitably arresting and strange artwork, across several pages of *Wired*. But that morning, the only audience was me, sitting alone with him in his living room.

There had always been a biblical element to Louis's saga—
he'd screwed up, and was therefore condemned to wander in
the desert. He might never enter the promised land, but the
young people he'd led out of bondage would cross over.

AND THEY were having a marvelous time, it seemed.

As responses to the geek columns continued to roll in, I
heard from a Texas minister whose website allowed his parish-
ioners to give him feedback on his sermons, and from an
Alaskan Inuit who ran her tribe's computer operations. Programmers, gamers, designers, and systems operators weighed
in with their tales of vindication, of a new order unfolding.
"We're building the pyramids of tomorrow," wrote JameB2.
"Ain't it cool?"

They thrilled to the great reversal: The suits were dependent
on them. Let the gatekeepers and moral guardians cluck and
caw about civilization crumbling. They loved their bold new
world and were filled with passion and enthusiasm about it.

They also celebrated the experience of finding one another.
They were almost painfully eager for community.

"The term 'geek' and the terribly powerful social and emotional stigma that accompanies the term had me running from
it," e-mailed Doug Riordan, an online developer. "Now I find
myself embracing what I am. I am my own geek."

One response stood out, from another correspondent who'd
become his own geek. I happened to be online late at night,
sorting through the geek outpouring, when an e-message appeared from a small town in southern Idaho. E-mail sometimes
has a peculiar chemistry all its own. Instantly transfixed, I had

the sense a writer sometimes gets when he's stumbled across the very thing he's been looking for.

Here was someone—a kid barely out of high school, Jesse Dailey—expressing surprise that his own experience with geek-hood was so widespread, even universal; he'd been stunned to recognize his travails—and also his triumphs—in my columns.

He'd written to tell me about a Geek Club that a sympathetic teacher had founded for Jesse and a few of his friends, and how the club had quickly become an institution at their rural school. The idea of a Geek Club in Middleton, Idaho, amazed me in itself. But I also responded to the kid's tone; his mixture of vulnerability, pride, and defiance.

I e-mailed him back and asked him to tell me more about himself.

He was a working-class geek who had done almost everything it was possible to do to and with a computer, and who'd graduated from high school a year earlier, Jesse wrote. He was working unenthusiastically but diligently in a small computer shop in dreary Caldwell. He shared an apartment with a classmate and fellow Geek Club alumnus, Eric Twilegar, who had a different kind of dead-end job: selling computers at Office Max in nearby Nampa. They spent most of their lives online, Jesse said, gaming, trawling for music, downloading free software.

The Geek Club—and this was where the triumph came in—had changed his life, he said, given him a place to belong, a name to call himself. Caldwell wasn't a particularly rewarding or stimulating place to live, he acknowledged, but that mattered less than it used to: He lived on the Net, which alone formed the boundaries of his life.

I'd been planning to crisscross the country visiting a number of the geeks who had contacted me. But after exchanging a few e-mails and phone calls with Jesse, I dropped that idea. I thought I'd found a better way to tell this story. I was soon on a plane to Idaho.

GEEKS

July 1999

I'm the "Head Geek" at my high school, which means that I work for the tech administrator doing IT-type work and coordinating the other work-study nerds. As you may imagine, we catch a lot of flak from other students because we spend so much time and energy on the computers at school, not to mention our own machines at home. When this happens, one of the things we do to shrug it off is to joke that if they didn't have us to keep their computers running, the school would cease to function. This is not altogether untrue.

Anyway, I was thinking about this tonight and watching *Dune,* the movie (it's a lot better if you've read the book, by the way). It occurred to me that what is true of my school is also true of other organizations, from small businesses to the federal government. Just like the Fremen in the movie stopped the universe by stopping the export of Spice, if computer geeks stopped working en masse, the whole country, and even the world, would grind to a halt.

How would this work though? Could some teamsteresque union (hopefully sans Jimmy Hoffa) work together on things that are important to us?

I figured you might be a good person to write to about this. You seem to get this kind of thing:).

—Aaron

1

FIRST ENCOUNTER

From: Jesse Dailey
To: Jon Katz

. . . It makes no sense to try, or even to want, to fit into a place where you don't belong. . . . It's not going to happen, and if it ever did, it's not what you would want anyway. . . . It's a delusion. The trick is to take something that's painful, and to make it so trivial that it's inconsequential. Just walk away and make it trivial. My advice to geeks? If you don't like it, leave, leave fast, make it trivial. Come to terms with who you are.

>   >   >

THE BOISE airport boasts several "fresh" French-fried potato vending machines, spaced at intervals throughout the facility, to let visitors know that they are in the proud Home of the Spud.

Caldwell is forty miles west, in the center of a flat plain known, for reasons that may have made sense long ago, as Treasure Valley.

Majestic mountains loom to the north, but they are a tease;

the Idaho of snowy peaks and ski resorts, plus a handful of militias and survivalists, is a long way off. This corner of southwestern Idaho is unrelentingly poor and plain, with vast stretches of empty roads and treeless farmland, intersected by equally vast swatches of fast-food franchises and car dealerships.

Driving into town in my rented car, I saw no obvious signs that Caldwell had ever prospered. It practically smacks you in the head with its barren agri-ugliness, its literal and architectural poverty, and its homogeneous Mormonness. The Church of Latter-Day Saints (LDS, to the locals), the dominant political, cultural, and social force, makes its presence seen and felt everywhere—on radio stations, in the newspapers, in education and business, in the ubiquity of church buildings, and the flow of ordinary conversation.

Stopping for coffee at a tiny restaurant near the center of town, I heard a waitress firmly quiet a customer who was mouthing off to a buddy about Monica Lewinsky: "Hush, we don't talk about that kind of thing in here."

Cruising the lifeless streets, I couldn't help thinking how tough it must be to be different here, because hardly anyone is. Residents are quick to acknowledge this: People who are restless, unusual, or ambitious get out quickly, sometimes heading for more forward-looking Nampa nearby, more often for booming Boise down the highway. I couldn't imagine a less hospitable place for a nineteen-year-old nonconformist.

The September heat was broiling but dry, under a desert sun. A layer of fine dust covered cars and roadways. I called Jesse at Emco Computers, where he worked.

"Hey," he said. No pleasantries, as in "Welcome" or "How was the trip?"

"Hey. Want to have lunch?"

"Sure. Stop by. I don't have a car. I ride my bike to work."

A surprise—in this open landscape, where the distance from home to work to a friend's place could easily be twenty miles, a car didn't seem like a luxury.

He gave me directions and a few minutes later I pulled into the parking lot of a small storefront on the town's Main Street. There was a green monitor painted on the outside window, along with hand-lettered signs offering repairs and software installations.

Tiny retail computer shops like Emco serve as a haven and gathering spot for idiosyncratic geeks, nerds, and techs who are miles from the nearest computer superstore and will never set foot in a lab at MIT or Caltech. Computers have replaced automobiles for a certain tribe of working-class American tinkerers who can never stop tweaking their machines and are constantly scrounging for new or used parts.

In a way, it made perfect sense that Jesse had a computer but not a car: Young Americans seem much more in love with their computers these days. The kid who might once have cruised through town showing off his new Mustang is more apt to invite friends over to see his turbocharged new hard drive.

Computers are cheaper and less greasy, but eternally evolving. Geeks' work is never done. There is no equivalent of the '56 Chevy, lovingly restored and meticulously maintained. Computers get outdated hourly. There are always better Net access, newer software, a continuous stream of updates, a more powerful hard drive, a by now incalculable inventory of gadgets and gizmos, programs, graphics, and operating systems.

Small shops like Emco, often started by techs who bristle at the idea of working for big corporations, are magnets for local geeks. They ultimately don't have a prayer, any more than the local five-and-dime can survive against Wal-Mart, though they try to find a niche by offering peripheral services, from repairs and wholesale parts distribution to servicing small business systems.

Still, it made sense that Jesse Dailey would have gravitated to a place like this, where he could use the gift he'd developed in grade school—taking computers apart and putting them together again. At his high school graduation a year earlier, a classmate, a son of Emco's owner, had approached him with a vague job offer. Jesse, having no other real prospects, grabbed the chance. What better way to cruise the Net and the Web, his work and his play as long as he could remember, than on somebody else's phone line?

ERNIE, THE owner, seemed to be expecting me and gestured to the repair bay in the rear of the store. Emco's tech department had the dimensions of a good-sized bathroom, with three or four desks where Jesse, the senior man, and a couple other techs replaced hard drives, added memory chips, assembled PCs, and resuscitated tired or fried modems.

Ernie looked a bit surprised to see that Jesse must have been telling the truth—some writer guy from New York had met him on the Net and had actually come all the way to Caldwell to talk to him. In fact, I anticipated that I might have to overcome some wariness from Jesse's employer, or puzzled colleagues, or cautious family members urging him to be careful. He was only a year out of high school, after all.

It was the first but not the last time I toted along my middle-class notions about parenting, only to learn that Jesse had been almost completely on his own for years.

The boomer ethos in which I'd raised my own daughter was obsessively protective, perpetually on guard against everything from lead paint and genetically engineered food to helmetless bike-riding, drinking, smoking, sex, and possible learning disabilities. Strangers, of course, represented the greatest danger of all—and in my mind, I was the classic stranger on the Internet, one of the central media-stoked phobias in American life, winging in from parts unknown to visit a nineteen year old who had no real idea whether I was who I said I was, or was doing what I said I was doing.

But Jesse's world was different. Hardly any of the decisions he made had involved consultation with or the supervision of adults.

It wasn't a question of estrangement—Jesse was quite close to members of his family, fractured though it was—but of a different value system. In Idaho, once you could take care of yourself, you did. You separated not the way upper-middle-class boomers' kids did, gradually and in long and expensive stages, but abruptly, usually irrevocably. It was understood that life involved dangers, but that kids learned how to handle themselves.

Emco had only one phone line, astonishingly, and Ernie's son was on it playing a computer game. His father turned to gently remind him that the store took business calls on that line. Otherwise, the place was quiet.

Around the corner of the front counter, a skinny, unsmiling kid looked up from a littered table and nodded, meeting my eyes only glancingly, then looking away. His face was void of expression, a mask I came to know well and could rarely crack. Jesse was taking apart a motherboard—the guts and circuits of a computer. He told me he'd be with me in a minute.

He was pale, his complexion like the underbelly of a fish, and he wore black-rimmed glasses. He had slightly stooped shoulders, as if his spine and neck had frozen in place after too much time hunched over a keyboard. He wore a red "Emco Computers" polo shirt, brown pants, and black Nike Airwalks.

I waited a few minutes, as he silently put the board together and told Ernie he'd be back in an hour.

WE SAID little as we drove past a string of modest prairie houses into Caldwell's fading downtown, except that Jesse pointed out several landmarks where he'd brushed up against the law. Here, he'd been stopped and searched while riding his bike. There, he'd been busted for driving under the influence. Over there, he'd hung out with some members of a gang he'd briefly joined.

This was the first manifestation of what I came to learn was bedrock Jesse ideology: He distrusted almost all authority and bureaucracy. Institutions—government, religion, school administrations, the music industry, Microsoft—were roadblocks, put on earth to obstruct and torment him, invade his privacy and limit his freedom of movement on the Internet. They were barricades to be circumvented, and he was part of a growing guerrilla force that knew how.

Downtown Caldwell had a sun-blasted Western feel. Half the stores on the wide street seemed to be pawnshops and check-cashing agencies, and the other half were shuttered.

Jesse had picked the town's only Chinese restaurant, run by white Mormons, he said. On cue, a severe-looking elderly white woman with blue-rinsed hair came to take our order. The food was, of course, dreadful. The Mexican place was better, Jesse said, but this one was farther from work, more private.

We were about as different as two American males could possibly be. I was a middle-aged bald guy more than thirty years older than he, a lifelong easterner. Jesse knew me as a writer for *Rolling Stone, Wired,* and Hotwired, the former website of the *Wired* empire, and that seemed to be enough. He knew nothing about my personal life as a father and husband and seemed utterly uninterested in my background as a former newspaper reporter and editor, TV producer, and professor turned media critic and author. What mattered was the context in which we had come together: the Internet.

Jesse was nineteen, a graduate of Middleton High, in an even smaller and emptier town a few miles away. Through his parents' various marital split-ups, he'd moved repeatedly from one remote and inhospitable town to another, learning to negotiate a series of stepparents along the way. He'd lived mostly in Montana until his mother decided to go to college to become a social worker and sent him to live with his father and stepmother for high school.

When Jesse decided to talk, which generally took a while, he had plenty to say. He was almost shockingly bright. Before we left the restaurant an hour and a half later, we had argued about *Wired* magazine, social responsibility, Charles Dickens, the future of the Net, and the definition of a geek; we'd discussed the *Star Wars* trilogy, the power of Bill Gates, the impact of the Web on big business, and the quality of various operating systems. We'd tackled gun control, the meaning of intellectual property, the structure of American education, and the future of networked computing.

We also began what was to be a running debate—and joke—on the subject of whether or not Jesse was intense, a word that came to mind. "No, that's not right," he challenged. "I wouldn't say intense. I'd say that I have 'clarity of intent.' "

As the check came, I couldn't help wondering about a central question, especially given that my daughter was up to her neck in the highly fraught college admissions process and had visited half a dozen campuses. "Why the hell aren't you in college?" I almost blurted.

He shrugged. "It wasn't anybody's expectation," he said. "It never really came up."

Did he have a lot of friends? I asked. He smiled, shook his head. Did he travel much? Never. Spend a lot of time outside? Only to ride his bike around. Had he hated high school? Completely, except for the members of the Geek Club and one or two teachers, especially Mr. Brown, the English teacher who had founded and named the Club. How did he get along with the Mormons who dominated this part of the world? Poorly. He'd taunted them repeatedly in school, arguing that the idea

of God and of organized religion in general was very nearly insane. But then, he hadn't gotten along with preppies or jocks either, or with the school's administrators. He had disrupted
commencement ceremonies by deliberately wearing a gold cap
and gown, and the principal had threatened to bar him unless
he changed into the mandated blue ones.

Did he know what he wanted to do in life? Sure. Work with
computers.

We talked a bit more, and then I asked him if he was as alone
as he seemed. He seemed startled by the question.

"I have the Internet," he tried to explain. "The Net is my
safety. It's my community. It's not a substitute for life for me. It
is life."

We agreed to meet later, with Eric, after work. They had
some business to transact.

I WAS coming to recognize the unmistakably heartland brew of
diesel fumes mixed with manure and restaurant exhaust. A stiff
wind blew dust through the air. Grinding engine noises from
passing trucks only partly drowned out the mournful bellowing
of some doomed cattle just a few yards down the road. As the
broiling sun set, a different kind of American landscape lit up:
The halogen floodlights from the truck stop could be seen for
miles.

In the dusk, two Diamondback Sorrento mountain bikes
flashed down past the Caldwell exit ramp from Highway 20–26,
past a dingy cowboy bar, a pizza place, a gun store.

Past, too, a towering marquee-like sign built by local politician Ralph Smeed to greet visitors to Caldwell. Tonight, its

black letters somewhat cryptically read: COLLEGE PROFESSORS ARE SMARTER THAN THE CAPITALISTS—PROFESSORS DON'T GIVE MONEY TO PEOPLE WHO HATE THEIR GUTS. The two guys on bikes paid little attention.

They pedaled along the edge of the lot, past parked cars and then back into the shadows, stopping suddenly next to a battered red pickup. One of them handed the driver something that looked like a laminated ID card, and the driver handed over something that looked like folded bills, then waved and drove off.

It was my second look at Jesse, still in his Emco Computer shirt, but my first at Eric, who appeared much more the Idaho farm kid than the classic geek. He was muscular, stocky, and short, with a black beard and blazing eyes. In contrast to Jesse's articulate ruminations about the Net and the World Wide Web, Eric was very nearly mute. He spoke only when spoken to and said as little as possible in response, except—he and Jesse were alike in this—when the subject was programming, computers, or any possible social or technical Net application.

Even though they'd come five or six miles, Jesse and Eric were barely sweating. They biked more than a hundred miles each week to see friends, visit their families, or pick up fast-food dinners at the Taco Bell down the road. They rode to and from work each day, Eric to the Office Max ten miles away in Nampa, Jesse to Emco's storefront.

They were on bikes because a few weeks earlier, Eric's '82 Olds sedan, their only other means of transport, caught fire on the highway to Nampa for the fourth or fifth time. The grease under the hood built up and ignited, and this time they were too far from fire extinguishers to put out the flames. They didn't even bother to call the fire department.

Afterward, they thoughtfully pushed the old clunker into a nearby junkyard with a note, but the owner declined the gift—the Olds had 185,000 miles on it—so they had to pay another guy to come tow it. The end of the Olds not only meant lost mobility, but the end of Eric's brief stint at Boise State University as well. He was trying to attend school and work full-time, but without any wheels, that was no longer possible.

They'd rather bike anyway, Jesse and Eric insisted. Biking was simple, inexpensive, paperwork-free, and different, something that set them apart, not that they needed anything more.

Besides, the car fire had inaugurated one of the most important discussions of both their lives, a talk that went on for hours, interspersed between ferocious Quake II battles on their linked computers.

"We saw the loss of the car as an opportunity," Eric recalled later. "We thought, hey, we have no car, dead-end jobs, no money—all we've really got are these technical skills. Because we knew computers, we figured we had a shot at getting out. There wasn't anything to hold us, especially without the car."

It turned out I'd played an unwitting role in this decision. During one of my preliminary telephone conversations with Jesse to set up this visit, he'd lamented the poor quality of life in Caldwell, and I'd asked him why he didn't move.

He seemed amazed at the question. "What do you mean?"

"Well, there's almost no unemployment among geeks," I told

him casually. "Geeks can get jobs almost anyplace. People everywhere need people who can maintain, repair, and understand computer systems. It's a universal need, don't you think?"

I thought Jesse was skeptical of the idea—he hadn't said two words in response—but he immediately did what I later learned was his almost stock response to any notion, question, or suggestion. He went online, cranked up a search engine, started browsing. He hopscotched electronically around the country, hour after hour for days, browsing through the help-wanted ads on newspaper websites in dozens of American cities.

Jeez, he told Eric. Katz is right. We can go anywhere we want. Let's get the hell out of here.

July 1997

Years ago the geeks would never have been tolerated in the corporation. You played by the rules of the bureaucracy or you didn't play at all. Several things have conspired, though, to make them more palatable. The bureaucracy is less entrenched and the workplace is more diverse.

Corporate life is no longer the white Anglo-Saxon male in a white shirt and dark tie. If you are going to be working with women, blacks, gays, and people from every country on earth, does the geek really stand out as much? The rules are different now. In addition, the pace of technology has made it almost impossible to keep up unless you are at least a little geeky. If you want to compete today you had better have a few geeks on your staff.

—Mark

THE CAVE

From: Jesse Dailey
To: Jon Katz

When I was looking on the Tribune, there were 433 jobs under Computer/Info Systems, under every other category I looked in there was an average of 15–20. . . . A total of about 40% computers. The problem now isn't finding a place in which those jobs are in demand, because like you say . . . they are everywhere. The problem is finding a place that wants to hire someone like me. In a Human Resources kinda way I'm defined as 19 w/ one year of experience. . . . In reality, I am an ageless geek, with years of personal experience, a fiercely aggressive intelligence coupled with geek wit, and the education of the best online material in the world. Aarrgghh!! too much stress being a geek on the move.:)

>   >   >

JESSE AND Eric lived in a cave—an airless two-bedroom apartment in a dank stucco-and-brick complex on the outskirts of Caldwell. Two doors down, chickens paraded around the street.

The apartment itself was dominated by two computers that sat across from the front door like twin shrines. Everything else—the piles of dirty laundry, the opened Doritos bags, the empty cans of generic soda pop, two ratty old chairs, and a moldering beanbag chair—was dispensable, an afterthought, props.

Jesse's computer was a Pentium II 300, Asus P2B (Intel BX chipset) motherboard; a Matrix Millennium II AGP; 160 MB SDRAM with a 15.5 GB total hard-drive space; a 4X CD-recorder; 24X CD-ROM; a 17-inch Micron monitor. Plus a scanner and printer. A well-thumbed paperback—Katherine Dunn's novel *Geek Love*—served as his mousepad.

Eric's computer: an AMD K-6 233 with a generic mother-board; an S3 video card, a 15-inch monitor; a 2.5 GB hard drive with 36 MB SDRAM. Jesse wangled the parts for both from work.

They stashed their bikes and then Jesse blasted in through the door, which was always left open since he can never hang on to keys, and went right to his PC, which was always on. He yelled a question to Eric about the new operating system. "We change them like cartons of milk," he explained. At the moment, he had NT 5, NT 4, Work Station, Windows 98, and he and Eric had begun fooling around with Linux, the complex, open-source software system rapidly spreading across the world.

Before settling in at his own rig, Eric grabbed a swig of milk from a carton in the refrigerator, taking a good whiff first. Meals usually consisted of a daily fast-food stop at lunchtime; everything else was more or less on the fly. There didn't seem to be any edible food in the refrigerator, apart from a slightly discolored hunk of cheddar cheese.

Jesse opened his MP3 playlist (MP3 is a wildly popular format for storing music on computer hard drives; on the Net, songs get traded like baseball cards) and pulled down five or six tracks—Alanis Morissette, John Lee Hooker, Eric Clapton, Ani DiFranco. He turned on his Web browser, checked his e-mail, opened ICQ chat (an also–rapidly growing global messaging and chat system) looking for messages from Sam Hunter, fellow Geek Club alumnus, or his mother or sisters.

He and Eric networked their computers for a few quick rounds of Quake II. Racing down hallways and passages on the screen, picking up ammo and medical supplies, acquiring ever bigger guns and blasters, the two kept up their techno-patter about the graphics, speed, and performance of their computers. "My hard drive is grungy," Eric complained. Jesse gunned Eric down three times in a row, then yelped, "Shit, I'm dead." A laser burst of bullets splattered blood all over the dungeon-like floor.

Meanwhile, the two of them continued to chat with me over their shoulders, pausing every now and then to kill or be killed. All the while, Jesse listened to music, and answered ICQ messages. Somebody called and asked about ordering an ID card, the cottage industry that at fifty bucks a pop will help underwrite their contemplated move to Chicago. Somebody e-mailed a few additional MP3s; somebody else sent software and upgrades for Quake and Doom. I was dizzied and distracted by all the activity; they were completely in their element.

The game was still under way when Eric moved over to the scanner and printer and printed out something semi-official-looking.

"Too dark," was Jesse's assessment, without seeming to look away from the screen. So Eric went back to his computer and called up a graphic program. Jesse took another phone call, still playing Quake, as Joni Mitchell gave way to Jane's Addiction, then the Red Hot Chili Peppers.

At any given point, he was doing six things almost simultaneously, sipping soda, glancing at the phone's caller ID, watching the scanner and the printer, blasting away at menacing soldiers, opening mail from an apartment manager in Chicago, fielding a message from his sister in Boise.

He wasn't just a kid at a computer, but something more, something new, an impresario and an Information Age CEO, transfixed and concentrated, almost part of the machinery, conducting the digital ensemble that controlled his life. Anyone could have come into the apartment and carted away everything in it, except for the computer, and Jesse wouldn't have noticed or perhaps cared that much. He was playing, working, networking, visiting, strategizing—all without skipping a function, getting confused, or stopping to think.

It was evidently second nature by now, which explained why he looked as if he hadn't been out in the sun for years. It was more or less true: A couple of weeks earlier, he'd gone hiking along the Idaho River on a bright day and landed in the hospital emergency room with his arms and legs severely sunburned.

He carried himself like someone who expected to get screwed, who would have to fend for himself when that happened, and who was almost never surprised when it did. Trouble, Jesse often declared, was the building block of character. Without the former, you didn't get the latter.

Of the two, Jesse was more social, more outward-looking. He sometimes read novels or, when he had no other means of communication, yakked on the phone (though almost always while online); he was on the lookout for a few good friends, though not highly sanguine about finding any. Eric rarely socialized, e-mailed, or chatted, at least about non-techie topics. Jesse claimed that if his computer were ever stolen or unplugged, he would read obsessively; Eric didn't know what he would do, and hoped never to find out.

Both had had difficult adolescent lives, in complex families under unstable circumstances. Eric, who hadn't seen or spoken with his father in years, had emerged darker, angrier than his friend, a part of him beyond the reach of teachers, peers, and well-intended adults. Jesse, hooked on arguments and ideas— he often describes himself as a fighter—could usually be drawn out of his shell.

Although they were forever getting into raging late-night debates about the nature of cable modem access, the longevity of Microsoft, or what constituted pass interference, and despite enormous philosophical and social differences, the two saw the world in essentially the same way.

That was, they were outsiders. They'd spent virtually all their nineteen years on the periphery of various things—families, teams, churches, school cliques—and had developed a profound suspicion of hierarchies, authorities, institutions, bureaucracies, and anything connected with them. Those things represented the other world, the road not taken, the domain of suits and yuppies. This shared philosophy, plus their mutual poverty, prompted them to rent the Cave together a year earlier. They might as well be broke and isolated together.

At times hurt and anger radiated from them like heat rising from Idaho blacktop in the sun. You could practically see the scars left by years of rejection and apartness. "I never went to one single high school party until graduation," Jesse told me once. "And if I'd been invited, I would've said yes, then not showed up. . . . I had that mutual inclination toward nerdiness." If Eric sometimes seemed to see this as his fate, a part of Jesse never quite accepted it.

Living with his divorced mom and two sisters in one Montana town or another, sometimes in dire poverty, Jesse always felt like an outcast. He grew up very much apart from the jocks who dominated the schools, the towns, his world. Sometimes his reading was to blame, sometimes his ponytail, sometimes his aversion to sports.

"He wasn't popular. He didn't have a lot of friends," his mother, Angela Dailey, recognized. "He was out cruising the cosmos with Stephen Hawking while the other kids were playing."

Despite the name of the club that so shaped them, there was nothing nerdy about Jesse or Eric. Both were tough, smart, resilient, and independent. In fact, before the Geek Club, Jesse had some ugly bouts with gangs and drugs, and several run-ins with local cops.

From the time he entered middle school, though, Jesse had also always had a computer—first a hand-me-down from someone he could no longer recall, then one left behind by his mother's departing boyfriend—and through them, his own portable and growing cyber-community. Perhaps he didn't really need the world of high school games and dances and crowds. He was too busy taking part in the creation of his own.

White, working-class kids are as invisible in media and politics as the poorest toddlers in the worst slums. They're nobody's children, really, nobody's constituency. Politicians don't worry about them and interest groups don't lobby for them. Thrown mostly on their own by divorce (four already among Jesse and Eric's families, with more possible) and by financial precariousness, Jesse and Eric knew the score: When you're out of high school, you're on your own. If you want more education, you work to pay for it. You find your own career track, or don't.

"For most of my friends, life is liquor, drugs, and bad jobs with no hope of escape," Jesse had told me. "That's what I grew up seeing. It's just life here, for some kinds of people." When he ticked off the names of friends he grew up with, it was a litany of trouble: one was an alcoholic and divorced at twenty, with a child and no job. Another, unemployed, was perpetually blasted on drugs. One lived from party to weekend party; he was in a beery stupor much of the time in between. They all worked at bottom-rung jobs in "big-box" superstores and fast-food franchises for $7 an hour.

For Jesse and Eric, therefore, getting out of Idaho was less a lifestyle choice than a matter of survival. There was no net beneath these kids, only the Net. It had guided much of their lives—how they thought, what they did, what kind of a future they could have. It was the only thing they trusted absolutely and relied on continuously. So far, it was one of the few things that had never really failed them. "The Net isn't work and it isn't play," Jesse explained. "It's work *and* play."

Not surprisingly, both harbored smoldering class resentment at people whose parents bought them computers and $100 pairs of Timberlands and unquestioningly paid for their college expenses. Unhappiness and suffering builds character, Jesse told himself—and me—again and again, repeating one of his Nietzschean mantras. What doesn't kill you makes you stronger.

They'd learned to expect little from bosses and other authority figures, with the single and crucial exception of a teacher named Mike Brown, whom they both credited with having changed their lives.

January 1997

Yeah, although I was considered a geek by most of the people throughout my high school years, I found that even geeks get laid in the '90s. . . . I have been working in Ho Chi Minh City, Vietnam, for about three years now and I am surrounded by geeks at work. The Vietnamese geek and the American geek are the same breed, containing the same amount of personality quirks you outlined in your articles. . . . I feel at times that this is the first time in the history of the world that geeks can really take charge. The faceless quality of the Net erases the problems geeks face in the "real" world of image, fashion, communication skills, etc. I foresee an International Geek Tribunal emerging through the vast slowly connecting networks that are already forming between geeks here and geeks there. Hopefully, it will help.

Thanks,
—Kirk

THE GEEK CLUB

From: Jesse Dailey
To: Jon Katz

In my junior year of high school, me and three of my close friends began to hold the meetings of what would soon become the infamous Geek Club. Perhaps "meetings" is too formal a word for this. It merely consisted of four of us, in the English teacher's (the local liberal) classroom, eating lunch every day and reveling in our self-imposed and self-indulgent segregation. By the end of my senior year, it had become a veritable institution. We had become quite well recognized by the school populus, it became a kind of running joke among all the people in our class, and for one of the first times, it wasn't a joke to which we were the butt, we were the ones delivering the punch line.

> > >

THIS WAS part of the first e-mail Jesse sent me, the one that sent me off to Caldwell to meet the author. He later described it as "a nuclear bit of e-mail," given the chain of events it subsequently triggered.

It was engagingly well-written, with a sense of irony and a nearly wicked wit, and it was strikingly self-aware for a nineteen year old.

Perhaps inadvertently, his message also reflected the transformation of geeks all over the world: They were suddenly the ones delivering the punch line. I saw that sense of ascent and transcendence expressed scores of times daily on the Net and the Web: That geekdom wasn't primarily about technology, it was about *using* technology to effect change—personally and often, albeit unconsciously, politically.

Jesse and Eric have a community and even a religion: The Net will provide. It will help them learn and grow, build new lives, find new friends (maybe even women).

My first day in Idaho, it struck me how strangely traditional and American their story was, and how simultaneously unprecedented: two unattached, semidestitute kids were planning to head cross-country, to leave their dreary lives behind and make their fortunes in a strange, huge, vastly more complex place than either had ever seen.

But instead of hopping a freight, it was the Internet they'd ride out of town to Chicago, and it was the Middleton High Geek Club that started the trip. Jesse and Eric were exactly 50 percent of its membership, along with Sam Hunter, just starting his first year at Albertson College of Idaho, down the road in Caldwell, and Joe Angell, a freshman at the University of Colorado. The only place in Idaho Jesse was insistent on showing me was their clubhouse—Mike Brown's classroom.

Middleton actually made Caldwell look urban; it was barely a town at all. We drove past farms, fading old houses, gas stations, a couple of sandwich shops. Middleton High seemed frozen somewhere in the fifties, a sprawling, one-story tile, glass, and brick complex, many of whose students were headed inexorably toward lifetimes of low-paying jobs in small, conservative Idaho towns.

"The best you can do around here is to get to Boise State," said Eric, who had attempted that very thing, "then maybe get a computer job there. That's what getting out of Middleton usually means." Not that anybody here had ever pushed them to get out, told them they were smart enough to, or offered much help. There was only Mr. Brown, the genial, stocky, sandy-haired English teacher from New York—official school liberal, magnet for and friend of outcasts.

From the moment Jesse and Eric approached the school, and even more so as they crossed the parking lot, walked through the door and down the hallways, they turned wary and alert. They glowered at the LDS Church that sits right next to Middleton High. Non-Mormon as well as Mormon kids are given time in their school schedules—the kids call it going to "seminary"—to visit nearby Mormon churches daily.

A handful of kids said hello in the halls; Jesse and Eric nodded, but didn't stop for conversation. It wasn't exactly a joyous homecoming.

The three of us showed up in Mr. Brown's room at about noon, just when the Geek Club used to convene, Jesse and Eric drifting to their usual seats in the far corner of the classroom.

"We're getting out of Idaho," Jesse told him, after they'd introduced me. "We're going to Chicago."

"Wow," said Brown, a bit surprised. "Great news."

Mike Brown was a warm, easygoing guy, not only the founder of the Geek Club, but one of the school's football coaches. He was also, it was clear, one of those teachers who genuinely enjoys kids. He had the gift of tapping into the rebellious streak of a kid like Jesse while simultaneously curbing and channeling it.

Everyone in the Geek Club used the same phrases—"a truly great teacher," Sam Hunter said—to describe Mr. Brown. He was the person—sometimes the only person—who made them think and listened to their ideas. He was funny, accessible, self-deprecating, and informal—unusual qualities at Middleton High, where geeks were not beloved, and where Jesse still bitterly recalls a teacher who punished students for goofing off by making them compose papers on a classroom typewriter—a typewriter!—instead of a computer.

Most teachers avoided controversial subjects, but Mr. Brown's classroom reverberated with them. "Horrendous debates over everything from evolution to abortion," Joe Angell said. "Sometimes it split along Mormon and non-Mormon lines. We talked about politics. He encouraged me to read *Catch-22*, and it's my favorite single book."

Among his students, Jesse and Eric and Sam and Joe stood out; they were all idea-starved. "I could see they needed a place to talk, a refuge here. A place to feel safe," Brown recounted, as I wedged myself into a chair with a writing arm. "They weren't jocks or preps, the dominant social groups. They liked to kick around ideas, argue about movies and books. Sam and Joe were less vehement, though, and better-liked by their peers. Jesse and Eric never seemed to care much about being liked."

In fact, Eric Twilegar personified the social attitude of the hard-core geek—distance, anger, alienation. And Jesse Dailey was the school's official Mormon-baiter, no insignificant role in these parts, challenging the existence of God and the validity of dogma, criticizing the values and tenets of LDS without fear— or much tact or respect, either.

Perhaps it was inevitable that Jesse, a memorable figure in a trench coat who wore a corduroy porkpie hat over his shoulder-length hair, would come to define himself—and be defined by his peers—as the Other.

"He was wild," one of Sam's friends told me. "He loved to argue, especially about religion, but he'd fight about anything, especially if it would tick off the preps who ran the school or the Mormons. He was the only one of his kind around here, somewhere between a prophet and a hippie preacher." Some of the Mormon kids, intent on saving Jesse, brought him notes from their bishops and copies of the Book of Mormon to try to win him over. They didn't have a prayer.

It was 1996 and Brown had been reading Katherine Dunn's strange, evocative novel *Geek Love,* talking about it in class, pointing out the enthusiastic alienation of its characters. "The book takes the extreme case," Brown recalled. "People as far on the fringes as you can get, completely dehumanized by 'normal' society. And it humanizes them—which is ironic, because they're already human."

At first, when the four boys began drifting in awkwardly at lunchtime, Brown was afraid to spook them. Deliberately, he barely looked up from the papers he was grading as Sam, Jesse, Eric, and Joe, foregoing the theater of hostilities that was the cafeteria, carried bag lunches into his classroom and spent the period arguing about movies and books and, increasingly, about computers.

"They always sat in the farthest corner," Brown said. "Gradually, we talked as I worked and they ate."

All four had grown passionate about computing and the Internet. Sam and Joe had become the school's roaming tech support, a rapidly spreading phenomenon among geeks as hard-pressed and technophobic school districts turned to their onetime social outcasts to help run their computer systems. In fact, geeks repeatedly cite the nearly universal need for people who can cope with computers and software as the primary reason for their elevation to a new techno-elite.

If Sam and Joe had turned their new interest outward, Jesse and Eric characteristically went the more solitary route, obsessing over hardware, code, hacking, and games.

Brown sensed that Jesse, in particular, was in distress, but didn't know exactly what kind; Jesse never talked about personal stuff. Brown didn't know that the year before, Jesse had joined a street gang in nearby Nampa, had been shot at late one night by a rival gang member, had gotten into marijuana and amphetamines, and had been busted by the Caldwell police for driving under the influence of liquor and for possession of marijuana (the case was plea-bargained).

Jesse didn't volunteer much about that time to me, either. It lasted between six months and a year, he said a bit vaguely. The gang had about a dozen members, who hung out, smoked dope, and broke into cars. "A form of rebellion," he said. "I don't know what else to call it. It was as if I had to go down, all the way to the bottom, to the guts of things, before I could move on. I saw it as an exploratory time. I wrote a paper about it at the end of my junior year, but I lost it."

In March 1995, the *Idaho Statesman* had run an article about the so-called phenomenon of Internet addiction. Jesse, then sixteen and described as a "supersmart teen," figured prominently in the story, saying he spent thirty-five to forty hours per week online. "It's like a revolution," he told the *Statesman*. "Being online sets you apart somehow; you can just log on and leave the world."

This is perhaps the most orienting part of the geek experience for many kids like Jesse: They see the Net as a separate world, *their* world.

"If you knew him, you knew the only thing he really cared about by the end of high school was the Internet," an old friend agreed. "Slowly, he had left the high school world behind, stopped caring about it. One-on-one, he is charming, considerate, loyal. But when you put him in the high school setting, it would just sometimes enrage and inflame him. He would take on anybody and everybody, especially when it was hopeless."

Mostly, Brown tried to channel Jesse's evident anger and frustration into constructive discussion.

Some kind of turning point arose the day a couple of kids wandered into the room, took in the scene and asked Jesse and the others if they were brown-nosing, scoring points. Brown stepped in. "I said, wait a minute, you don't belong in here, have you paid your dues? And the kid says 'What is this?'

"I answered that this was the Geek Club. If you want to hang in here, fine, but you've got to bite a chicken's head off first, are you willing to do that? Live up to your convictions."

Jesse got the idea on the spot and pounced, announcing that this was a private club; the intruders couldn't come in because they were too well-dressed. "It was amazing," Jesse says. "All of a sudden, we were a club and we could keep other people out."

From: Jesse Dailey
To: Jon Katz

Their names were Don and Kristin, they were two people whom I considered quite popular all through my younger years at school. . . . They jokingly said they'd like to join. I laughed and looked at Don's shoes, and said, "No, you can't be in here with shoes that cost that much." He asked why, and I told him it was because they were too trendy. It was a very short conversation, however, because I cut him off by asking him to recite pi to the sixth digit, claiming it was an entrance requirement, regardless of the shoes. Of course he couldn't do it and had to leave. But who could, except a geek?

For years, we had watched them go to parties, and always have a dance partner at the school dances, and always stand in the hall with four or five other people who liked, or at least pretended to like, them. And now that we had finally found our place to rest, our place to gather and be surrounded by ideas and people that we liked, and who liked us. . . . They wanted in . . . I think we all unspokenly agreed when they came in that in order to maintain our solidarity we had to stand up against the kinds of ideals that had plagued us for years.

I talked with Kristin about it a year or two later and she was honestly hurt by it. She honestly felt excluded and left out, unwanted and denied. I tried to make it clear to her that the feeling she had for that moment, we had been having for years because of the way in which her social group operated. I don't think she quite understood it though. She just couldn't quite get a hold of the pain that comes from having that happen nearly every day for years. I gave up very quickly trying to make people understand what it meant to be the outsider. I just quit caring. The concepts of inside and outside became trivial once I wanted them to be.

Afterward, Brown could see a change in all of them, but especially Jesse and Eric. "Suddenly, they had some power. It was fun. Some preps would walk in, and they would give it to them, tell them they weren't invited unless they were willing to become geeks. They had a way to fight back."

Jesse was conscious of a change in himself, as well. He had allies; it made him less angry.

His mother, now a clinical social worker living and practicing in Choteau, Montana, was enormously grateful. "The Geek Club saved Jesse in some ways," she believed. "The teacher saved him . . . Mr. Brown. I knew about the gang and the drugs, but I couldn't help him. He was always too smart for everybody, always rejected by the jocks, almost always on his own. But I could never convince him how smart he was. All of a sudden, he got into the Geek Club, and they had a community. They belonged."

In one sense, Angela Dailey was wrong. Jesse did hear her. "I remember my mom telling me how smart I was, and I guess I knew I was smart. I had a lot of other problems, but I never thought I was dumb. That got through to me."

For the first time, however, he had a name for himself, one he thought fit. He dropped out of the gang, stayed out. Geek-hood gave him a way to define himself, a way to be apart and feel okay about it, a way to value his brains and talents and, for good measure, a way to wreak a little vengeance.

From: Jesse Dailey
To: Jon Katz

There is sometimes a lot of pain in being a geek. When I first started using the name, it started to fit and at the same time empower. Calling myself a geek was saying to all the people who sometimes made me feel tortured, or isolated, or de-feated, "I don't care if you think I'm a two-headed freak. I think I'm better than you and smarter than you, and that's all that matters . . ."

Once he realized, more than a year later, that *geek* was even more than empowering slang, that it meant something con-crete, including the emerging reality that geeks could go pretty much anywhere they wanted and find a zero-unemployment rate, he knew that he had to leave.

GEEK VOICES

June 14, 1999

Katz,

I was trolling the Internet in search of something with some real content, not just a bunch of flashy graphics, when I came across an article you wrote entitled "Defining Geekdom." I found it very interesting . . .

   I too am a geek and quite proud of it. . . . I recently sold my car to buy a laptop. Having sold my car I realized that the mobility a laptop provides is somewhat unnecessary if you don't go anywhere. Oh well, keep up the good work.

—Keal

LEAVE FAST

From: Jesse Dailey
To: Jon Katz

I get about half my music from unprotected sites, and half from private sites with very restricted access. It's not getting "in" to the sites that is the problem. Children can do that. It's finding and getting to the physical place in which these servers reside, something impossible in the scheme of things, they can exist scattered all over the country and you would never know it. . . . For the consumer, it is a godsend, as he is no longer required to pay outrageous prices for music that may end up being bad.

In short, fuck the labels. Long live the music.

> > >

THEY'D GIVEN notice at work, told their landlord they were history, reserved a Ryder truck. To save rent, they'd spend their last couple of days living in an abandoned shack on Jesse's father's property. There was some packing to do, a farewell party a few friends were throwing tonight, some games of Doom and

Quake, a handful of good-byes to say—not an elaborate leave-taking.

Richard Dailey, Jesse's father, had a small ranch house outside Middleton. He'd taken a leave from his job as a town fire inspector after he was diagnosed with Parkinson's disease. The only outward signs of his disease, though, were the tremors in his hands and an occasional grappling for the right word. He was lean, a warm smile etched on his face, frail and shy.

The two were comfortable together, when Jesse stopped by to visit and to introduce this strange writer guy, but said very little. Jesse's stepmom was working in the kitchen; Eric hung silently in the background.

Richard Dailey passed around a scrapbook he kept, mementos from his own life and some childhood snapshots of Jesse and his sisters, from the days when the family was intact. The young Jesse—seen largely in photos of camping and riding trips up north—looked remarkably like the older one, grave and intent. Richard had also saved a magazine story about how he got caught in a vicious blizzard years ago and survived—saving his companions, too—by killing his horse and climbing inside its steaming carcass for warmth.

It's clear that there's a cowboy streak in the Dailey line. "Riding is something my dad and I did a lot of together," Richard says. He's most at ease talking about the past, the trips, hikes, and rides. But those were a couple of divorces and a serious illness ago, and the son looking over his shoulder at the mounted snapshots now had little in common with the boy in the pictures.

How did Richard feel about Jesse's looming departure for

Chicago? "Okay," he said, nodding. "Good." He paused for a bit. A part of him seemed to be struggling with the whole idea. "The only thing is, I hear it's cold up there. Jesse doesn't like cold weather. He might not last the first winter. If anything sends him home, it will be the cold."

Richard had given Jesse a few hundred dollars—not a small contribution under the circumstances—for the trip. Otherwise, Jesse said, the two of them never discussed it much. Once Jesse decided to go, there wasn't much to say. The same was true of his mother, with whom he spoke frequently and somewhat more openly. "I told my parents I was unhappy with my life and was forging ahead. We never talked about it much after that."

Now, as father and son sat down at the kitchen table with a map, if either felt conscious of a family about to split apart for good, there was no reference to it. Richard was trying to be helpful the best way he could, with advice about the journey it-self. Both knew there wouldn't be much help available, from any source, once Jesse got to far-off Chicago.

The senior Dailey had talked with a friend who'd recently driven east and warned about some construction along the way. He suggested a couple of route changes; Jesse marked them conscientiously on his map.

BACK AT the Cave, they had stuff to do in the days before they decamped, but not as much as one might think. There were a few last IDs to crank out, to earn an extra bit of road money. Eric, suddenly remembering that he had to drain his water bed, borrowed a length of rubber hose from a neighbor, stuck one end in the water bed nozzle and sucked out a mouthful of water, then spit it into the bathtub. "Jeez, water-bed water," he gasped. "Guess there's a lot of chemicals in there." The water trickled out slowly into the tub. If the huge bed wasn't emptied within forty-eight hours, it would be left behind.

Jesse biked down to Emco for some boxes, but didn't really need many. Clothes would get stuffed into duffels and plastic garbage bags. There were the bikes, some books. The only thing they would actually pack carefully into boxes, at the last possible moment, were their two computers, along with monitors, hard drives, scanners, subwoofers, and printers. They would spend more time packing them than they would everything else they owned, combined.

Jesse had taken charge, with Eric happy to abide by his decisions. He didn't really care where they lived, as long as they found decent jobs, had good Net access, and met some computer types to hang out with. Programming was Eric's life. "It's the only thing I'm good at," he said, somewhat bleakly. He'd like to have a social life, especially a girlfriend, but that wasn't in the cards in Caldwell. Maybe in Chicago.

So it was Jesse who'd gone on the Web and, between bouts of Quake II, torn through various search engines and relevant Chicago websites. He made some phone calls, sent some faxes, memorized some online maps of neighborhoods and subways—but mostly he browsed on the Net.

He trawled for jobs on the *Chicago Tribune* site, on computer mailing lists and on geek employment agency websites. He checked out apartment rentals through

www.relconapartments.com and grabbed an affordable-sound-
ing, two-bedroom w/balcony on the train route in suburban
Richton Park, sight unseen.

To plan their route, he bought a Rand McNally TripMaker
CD, copied it, and then returned it to the store. Geeks do not,
as a rule, pay for things digital, except for products adjudged so
outstanding that their creators are deemed deserving of payment; they trade, borrow, copy ("burn"), or hack them instead.

Insofar as they are political at all, many geeks and hackers (a
term frequently misapplied, used for computer vandals and
thieves, but more accurately referring to computer problem-
solvers and tinkerers) share this principle: Keeping the Net
free from corporate and government control is a sacred task.
Getting stuff for free on the Net is a matter of pride, therefore,
a demonstration of determination, computing skills, and righ-
teous geek thinking.

Property, Jesse informed me, came in two varieties, material
and intellectual. You paid for the former, but almost never for
the latter. Geeks were, in fact, redefining conventional notions
of commerce and ownership.

Jesse had a music playlist hundreds of songs long, for instance, but couldn't remember the last CD he'd actually
purchased. He read news online, but rarely bought a newspaper or a magazine. Journalists, educators, and pundits
frequently fuss that kids like Jesse don't read or aren't well informed; in fact, they read enormous amounts of material online, and are astonishingly well informed about subjects they're
interested in.

Geeks were the first to grasp just how much information was available on the Web, since they wrote the programs that put much of it there—movie times and reviews, bus and train schedules, news and opinions, catalogues, appliance instructions, plus, of course, software and its upgrades.

And of course, music, the liberation of which is considered a seminal geek accomplishment.

Virtually everything in a newspaper—and in many magazines—is now available online. In fact, some things, like the latest weather and breaking news, appear online hours before they hit print.

Yet while Jesse had gone through literally thousands of downloaded software applications, he'd never paid for any of them. He didn't even quite get the concept. The single cultural exception was books. Perhaps as a legacy of his childhood, Jesse remained an obsessive reader. He liked digging through the bins of used bookstores to buy sci-fi and classic literature; he liked books, holding them and turning their pages.

"But you pay for material things," he explained. "I'd never pay for any software or music, but I'd never steal a TV from a store." He didn't consider acquiring free music online to be pirating or theft, though. Intellectual property belonged to everybody.

In fact, Jesse and many geeks consider themselves liberators of ideas and culture, using the Net to literally pry them from what they see as greedy corporations and powerful, censorious institutions. As mass media has grown corporatized—with journalism, publishing, moviemaking, and the music business

getting sold and merged into fewer and larger monoliths—
geeks feel ever more entitled to take whatever intellectual
property they want. The individual creators of this property—
writers, musicians, artists—can and will find alternative means
of generating income, they're convinced.

It's an enormous idea for a capitalistic country with long-
standing ideas about property and payment, and it's putting the
ascendant geek culture in increasingly direct conflict with such
institutions as the legal and medical professions, both of which
have vowed they will fight the notion of free, "open source" information on the Net.

So far, though, the geeks seem to be winning. They're bringing
the music industry to its knees, for instance. In the past few
years, stereos have begun disappearing from college dorms as
students attach speakers to their computers and play their MP3s.
Like Jesse, they use computers to distribute a growing variety of
information on subjects and in places to which access has long
been tightly controlled: legal and medical data, academic libraries, stock trading, films.

Jesse intuitively grasped the political implications. "No way
intellectual property will be controlled," he said. "It's just never
going to happen again."

Yet somehow, despite virtually living on the Net, the discovery that he physically could live in almost any city in the country had come as a shock, an awakening akin to joining the Geek
Club. He hadn't seen what he'd been doing for years—building
computers, writing code, playing games, installing complicated
software and operating systems—as something marketable or

valuable, something that offered status or options in the larger society. "I just didn't realize it until I got online. It just didn't occur to me," he said.

But once it did occur to him, it seemed to embolden him, even past the point of caution.

Jesse had been planning this campaign like Patton plowing through Europe. He knew nothing about cities or urban life, but he was convinced that he didn't really have time to find out and still meet his flight-from-Idaho schedule. He was tense, possessed, fearful that if he slowed or paused he might lose the courage or the momentum he needed to get out.

Jesse and Eric hadn't given a second thought to leaving since that "metaphysical moment"—as Eric put it—when they stood contemplating the smoldering wreck of his Olds. Jesse had computed how many paychecks they would get—two for him and four for Eric—if they waited a month before leaving. Pending a few breaks and no serious setbacks, that might be just enough. The only questions were where to go and how to get there.

His plow-ahead-and-cope philosophy came in handy here. When Jesse wants to go to a movie, he employs the Grand Unified Jesse Dailey Theory of Moviegoing: Simply head out the door on whatever means of transportation is available, come across the nearest theater, find a movie to see. He rarely showed up when a particular movie was about to begin, so he'd seen beginnings, finales, and middles of dozens of movies, but hardly any in their entirety. The *Star Wars* series was among the few exceptions. Something about this reflected his relentless need to beat all systems, whatever they were. Checking schedules was for suits and old farts.

He'd chosen Chicago in this way. It was a big city, and probably somewhere within it were jobs, apartments, and plenty of computer stuff. A headhunter he'd contacted via e-mail was practically guaranteeing them work.

As true geeks, it was almost a point of pride to avoid one of the trendy enclaves most American kids would kill to get to. "We thought about Seattle or San Francisco, or Boston," Eric said, "but no way do we want to go to yuppie cities." In one way or another, Jesse and Eric had been battling those hipsters their whole lives; they were not about to move across the country just to get rejected again by people who might call themselves geeks but wore hundred-dollar shoes.

Chicago, they had heard (where? online, naturally) was a working-class town, with a reputation for unpretentiousness, not privilege. Neither of them had ever set foot in Chicago or met anyone else who had. But that was par for the course, Jesse pointed out. "You get used to it. You don't have parents writing checks, networks of people from college. You live off the Net and the Web. You really live there. You use the technology; you make it work for you."

After all this research, he had worked up a slightly unnerving spreadsheet and kept a copy tucked into his wallet. It had two columns. Under "What We Need" was $680 a month for rent, $130 for phone, $100 for utilities, $130 for transportation. If they ate only once or twice a day at $3.33 per meal, that totaled $1,640 a month, Jesse estimated.

Under "What We Have," he'd listed the $149.72 deposit that

would be returned by Ryder, plus cash reserves: Jesse, $1,072, and Eric, $481. In addition, the two were counting on another $481 in paychecks. They'd borrowed a little from relatives to pay the apartment deposit and to buy some clothes that seemed appropriate for a city (though, except for Eric's brief stay with a brother in Seattle the previous summer, Boise was the only city they'd ever been to).

Their safety net, money left over for emergencies and unforeseen expenses, came to $10.72.

THE PARTY was at Joe Allen's house, a split-level miles from their apartment but still in Caldwell. A friend had given Jesse and Eric a lift. The directions I had simply said to head down the Interstate, take a particular exit, find a certain road, and turn left. But I was driving for half an hour before I came upon any turn that could conceivably be called a road. I saw no houses or street lights, either, just a potato-processing plant that was bigger than many towns—the giant Simplot complex—and seemed to extend for miles.

Down a long, dark stretch of asphalt, I eventually came upon Joe's place, across the street from a barn and a pasture. The driveway was filling with Jeeps, a couple of pickups, and some small sedans.

Inside, Jesse was playing chess in one room with Sam's younger brother; I found Eric off by himself, drinking a beer in the playroom. Two sets of jocks were arm wrestling at the kitchen table. A GOOD LUCK, JESSE AND ERIC sign had been taped to the refrigerator door.

The party felt muted, unfocused, scattered all over the

house. Everybody was drinking. People came up sporadically to wish Jesse luck or say good-bye, but plainly found the trek a little bizarre, a typically Jesse thing to do. Considering the dimensions of the project, the departure caused rather little discussion unless I raised the topic. People almost seemed to be avoiding the subject.

Sam, who turned out to be decidedly non-geeky—he was blond, clean-cut and cheerful—thought that Jesse and Eric would do fine. But he wasn't drawn to move so far away from family and friends himself, he conceded. There might be prettier or more sophisticated places to live than Caldwell and Middleton, but few that felt more comfortable or were better places to raise a family.

"I think they're nuts, I guess," offered a clearly buzzed friend. "Idaho is safe, friendly. They might not be the most popular kids in the town, but they do have friends here. They've never been to a place like Chicago. Maybe they'll get eaten alive. It's scary. I hear it's crowded and ugly and dangerous."

Jesse laughed later when he heard that. "It isn't as scary as staying here," he said.

THE NEXT morning, a Sunday, was the last day in their apartment. Eric had biked off to Office Max to earn a few extra dollars. Jesse, sitting shirtless in front of his computer, had clearly just gotten up.

The Cave, which had never been especially homey, now looked like a typhoon had hit. Some of the computer peripherals were already in boxes, but clothes and household stuff and books were scattered through every room.

Jesse looked deflated, resigned, as if the wind had suddenly been knocked out of him after days of intense focus on the trip.

Last night's party had clearly been a bust. "It was a bit sad," he conceded, strong language from him. "Half the people, I didn't know." For Jesse—careful to avoid language that suggested emotion, never angry but "irritated," never hurt but "disappointed"—this came close to an expression of grief.

He had kissed one girl, somebody he'd been interested in for a long time; kissed her twice, in fact. But she'd told him she didn't want that kind of relationship. "My last stab at acceptance in Caldwell," he muttered.

I had been, to date, meticulously journalistic in my dealings with Jesse. I'd advised him repeatedly of his journalistic "rights," that anything he said could appear in print unless he specified otherwise. That he shouldn't do or say anything in my presence that he didn't want to see in a magazine or book. That while I would certainly be friendly, that didn't necessarily mean I was his friend.

I scrupulously avoided giving advice, even when he was recklessly indiscreet about the booming fake ID business going on in the apartment; even when I saw him fax off a signed rental agreement for an unseen apartment in a town I'd never heard of, one that didn't appear on the Chicago map or even have a Chicago area code.

In fact, much as I admired his planning and pluck, his trip seemed frighteningly ill-conceived. He had no cash reserves, and no people he could turn to who did. No car, in a climate where bikes might prove of limited utility.

They were headed for a melting pot, yet neither had spent much time around minorities, other than a few Mexican families who lived in Caldwell. The gang Jesse had joined once, while rough, was probably very different from the Chicago gangs I'd often read about.

Most importantly, there was no margin of error. If a single thing went wrong—the rental truck broke down, the apartment wasn't available, a job didn't materialize swiftly—Jesse and Eric didn't even have enough money to get back to Idaho.

Jesse didn't want to think about that. "This has got to work," he said. "This is where 'clarity of intent' applies. I really have no choice but to believe it will work. The second I stop believing that, I won't be able to do it."

By his own timetable, he had three weeks to travel to Chicago, get settled in a new apartment, land work, and cash a paycheck before he ran out of even enough money to take the subway. He shrugged. "Worst-case scenario? The money runs out and we live on the streets of Chicago. Or we call our parents and borrow $125 for the Greyhound. Given the two choices, I'd probably opt for the streets."

Were this my kid, I'd have been beside myself. But nobody in Jesse's family was sounding any alarms, and my role was to keep my mouth shut and take notes, to observe but not to interfere. The closest I'd come to violating that tenet had been a very subtle hint—which Jesse had ignored anyway—that getting an apartment in Chicago via the Net might prove risky.

Otherwise, I couldn't say or do anything that would affect the outcome of the story.

Besides, Jesse had absolute confidence in his computing skills, in his technology. The Net was a faith to him, an ideology. It had gotten him through the poverty and loneliness of a nomadic life in Montana, the pain of adolescence, the rejection and anger of high school. Once he'd grasped that there were jobs, he reasoned that he could compete with anybody when it came to getting one.

So he was setting off in a rented Ryder with a fake ID of his own, no credit cards, and ten bucks to fall back on if anything went wrong.

What made my detachment particularly difficult was how much I'd liked Jesse from our first online encounter. I appreciated his wily maneuvering on the Net, his bizarre sense of humor, his oddly defiant view of his world, his striking intelligence and lust for ideas.

Despite the obvious differences between us, there were also some connections. He was a lost boy. I'd been one myself, and we know one another when we meet. Lost boys have a strange kind of brotherhood.

We shared other traits as well, alas: He was rebellious and resentful of authority, quick to rage at arbitrary power. I had been too, for most of my life. While I wasn't a computer geek, I too loved the Net and the Web, and also could talk about both forever. We shared an oddly similar point of view about the world.

We'd already spent hours yakking into the night about computers, politics, education. Jesse's normally cautious veneer would peel away in a second at the appearance of an interesting idea or argument. His sometimes heavy-lidded, almost reptilian expression vanished; his eyes lit up, his arms would windmill, and his voice rise. We enjoyed sparring with each other.

And there was something else. My wife and I had lost our first two children; we'd decided to abort after prenatal diagnoses of a rare but invariably fatal genetic disease. On our third try, we were luckier and had a daughter whom we adored.

In all the years since losing the boy we would have named Ben, I'd never met a kid and felt that he was something like the boy I imagined my son might have been.

I didn't want to be Jesse's father—he had one and wasn't looking for another, and I was somebody else's. But I had a striking sense that if I'd had a son, he would, at the core, be a lot like this brainy, combative oddball sitting in a musty apartment in a small Idaho town.

That morning, I talked to him about isolation and rejection, about how universal they were to people like him and like me, but how temporal they often were. High school wasn't life, I reminded him, just a small part of it.

I told him he was doing a brave thing; that he had many assets—intelligence and wit, good looks, personality—and that, as a computer geek, he was in the storied right place at the right time. This was the gold rush for geeks, a special time in history, the Internet moment, and he was primed to take advantage of that, to stake his claim. A couple of decades ago, his choices might have been the military or the Simplot plant or, if he were lucky, a trade or vocational school. He couldn't possibly have considered the kind of move he was about to undertake.

I saw him brighten as he leaned over the computer to fiddle with his music playlist. He looked at me closely, a rare thing. It was almost impossible for him to focus on anything else for too long when the computer was on, which it always was. Normally, you had to drag him out of the apartment to talk.

"I think you're right," he said. "I think, for the first time in my life, that things really can be different. They have to be different."

We talked for half an hour about changing outcomes, about whether directions in life can be altered or reversed. "Maybe somewhat," he said dubiously. "Not radically. You can't change who you are."

"I know this won't be easy," he added, as if he'd been reading my mind. "I know there are risks. But think about the risks if I stay here."

In Chicago, I told him, geeks were probably one of the least odd subcultures around. Nobody would care if he were a Mormon or a Jesuit or an Orthodox Jew, let alone a computer geek. Chicago had plenty of each, plus a lot more; there was some of everything there. He could start all over. He could build any kind of social life he wanted.

"Now that," he said, shaking his head, "that would be a radical change."

We said good-bye, agreeing that I would fly out to Chicago a couple of weeks after he and Eric had landed. I threatened all sorts of mayhem if he didn't write down details of the trip and e-mail them to me.

Then Jesse went to answer the phone—he was clearly cranking out as many last-minute IDs as possible to help finance the move—and I pulled $140 in twenties from my wallet and, in violation of every journalistic guideline, left the bills on his keyboard. Then I drove to the airport in my rental car and flew home. I knew I'd never set foot in Caldwell again, but I couldn't quite fathom whether Jesse ever would or not.

June 1998

In the late '80s, early '90s, I found myself gravitating toward wearing mostly black, not because it's what people were doing, but because I was studying kung fu and our uniforms were black. . . . I wasn't even aware it was a trend until I started running across references to "people in black" and such in news articles. My thoughts were something like, "Doggone it, why are they copying me? Now I've gotta change. . . ." [Being a geek] is a desire to be unique and the sense that if what I'm doing becomes trendy or faddish, then I want to go do something else. . . .

—Tom

THE TRIP

From: Jesse Dailey
To: Jon Katz

Hey Jon . . . I told you I'd tell you the story of Laramie, WY, and why I think it was all too fitting. Eleven o'clock Saturday night we are stuck (naturally) on the freeway for about an hour, so I forced myself to get out and walk around to stretch my legs and to try and start up a conversation with the two girls I had seen in the car in front of us. Now, this is not something that I would ever ever consider doing in the real world, but the whole trip already had a surrealistic pallor . . . as traffic began to clear they invited me to bring Eric and go back to their apartment and party with them and also to crash there since we couldn't find a hotel. We opted to bag the idea of driving all night and to accept their invitation.

When we arrived we were confronted with the age-old conflict of geek v. mainstream. We entered into what was a U of Wyoming college party on the local Saturday night, something that people our age do quite frequently, but that we do not. Immediately, I could tell that Eric was very uncomfortable and feeling very awkward, and I was not comfortable, but not

awkward either. I opted to put us both on the road almost immediately after we got there, to save both of us the pointless
aggravation and strain to try and fit into a foreign mainstream
group. I had realized that we had come to the point of no return, the point where it was harder to try and fit in, than it was
to strike out alone. . . .

> > >

BEFORE LEAVING Idaho, they'd asked the search engines
HotBot and AltaVista if there would be any construction delays
on the route they'd planned. AltaVista led them to an updated
map server that warned of major trouble near Salt Lake City.

So they changed their plans, driving straight through for two
days and two nights, east on I-84 to Pocatello, southeast on
Highway 30 over the Rockies and into Wyoming, then onto
I-80 somewhere near Rock Springs and straight east into
Chicago. The trip was a blur, and tougher than they had expected; the truck's cab was smaller than they'd planned, so it
was harder to rest. And there was no time or money for sight-
seeing.

They found a cheap motel just outside Chicago and then, as
soon as it was light, drove their huge Ryder to Richton Park. It
was a nightmare.

"We could hardly believe it," Jesse later told me, recalling
that first morning when they gazed up at a squat, ugly, four-
story apartment complex facing a suburban highway. Miles of
little split levels and stretches of mall-lined highways surrounded the place. The only destinations remotely within walking distance, aside from the train stop across the street with its

vast commuter parking lot, were a Dunkin' Donuts, a pizza par-lor, and a supermarket called the Eagle Country Market.

"We were stunned," Eric said. "It looked like Idaho. We wanted to go back. It was a good thing we didn't have the money."

If the Web was devastatingly efficient at displaying maps on a screen, it needed some fine-tuning when it came to capturing the scale and feel of a place. This wasn't the bustling metropo-lis they'd envisioned. The apartment Jesse had put a deposit on wasn't available; they had to take a smaller one. Worse, there was, it turned out, no cable modem access in Richton Park.

In Idaho, the two rarely saw an African American. Here, they were among the few whites in the neighborhood. It didn't bother them; what did was noticing that they were also the only kids for, it seemed, miles around.

Sherry, the job broker Jesse had been e-mailing, had an of-fice well north and west; it took them two hours to get there, first by train, then by bus and foot—including an unplanned detour when they got off the train at the wrong stop and wan-dered briefly into a rough quadrant of Chicago's South Side. Then, it seemed, the job prospect Sherry had lined up for Jesse was with a small computer consulting company in a suburb even farther away, and the job she thought she might have for Eric hadn't materialized at all.

"It was pretty sobering," Jesse reported. "Here, we had come all this way and we really didn't understand anything about where we were going. Everything was strange. The people were cold and unfriendly, the food was expensive, the apartment was way out in nowhere, and we had no way of getting near the job that I had thought I'd lined up, assuming there was a job."

Nor was the longed-for community anywhere in sight. "We were the youngest people around. We didn't have cars. We didn't have families. We didn't have a single friend. We were nineteen. Nobody who lived in the apartment was anywhere near our age. We were in a kind of a panic."

Perhaps the strangest thing about the new apartment, I thought when I arrived a week later, was how much like the old one it looked—bare, dim, lit by the glow of computer screens. It was almost unthinkable, but Jesse and Eric, at great expense, risk, and trouble, had re-created the look and feel of the Cave.

Shell-shocked as they were, there was hope: Sherry had lined up another job interview for Jesse. To be sure of arriving in the Loop on time, he set his alarm for 6 A.M.

He showered, groped around in the dark for his brown pants, a beige shirt, and his new Old Navy baseball cap. Eric was still asleep in the other bedroom. A little sunlight was just beginning to stream in around the blanket they'd hung in front of the sliding-glass patio door.

He tucked Eric's brown dress shoes into his backpack (Eric was twitchy about their getting scuffed, so Jesse wasn't supposed to put them on until just before the interview), along with the tie he was agonizing about whether or not to wear.

He was tense, rushed, distracted, praying this job would pan out. According to his worn, continuously revised spreadsheet, he and Eric had two weeks left to find work and get their first paychecks before this new life in Chicago crashed like some cheap computer. Plan A was to get a paycheck by early October, then pay the second month's rent and utilities and buy food.

There was no Plan B.

At least he could take the train from Richton Park downtown. It was a long ride, but easier than the bus-train combo Sherry's other prospect would have entailed. The National Futures Association, which monitors the country's booming commodities industry and uses a lot of computer auditing to do it, was looking for a tech in its Information Systems department, a job that paid a stunning $32,000. Jesse ran the zip codes through AltaVista—his and the office location's—and figured he had a fifty- to sixty-minute train ride into town, plus a fifteen- to twenty-minute walk.

"I hope this works out," he was murmuring, flitting around, getting ready. "If we eat crackers, I can stretch things another week or two. But we can't go much longer. And I'd sure hate to have to go back to Idaho, which I'd have to borrow money even to do, and try to get my old job back at Emco. I didn't come all this way for that."

He was worried about Eric, who he feared would become frustrated and depressed if he didn't get work soon. He was worried about what would happen to both of them if Eric didn't get work soon. Both would rather cut off limbs than ask their strapped families for more money.

Jesse was both excited and visibly rattled by Chicago. Figuring out the transit system and its schedules was the kind of problem-solving exercise he relished. But there were lots more difficult things to adjust to.

Chicago was overwhelming. There were no skyscrapers in Caldwell, thousands here. The entire state of Idaho had one area code; the Chicago metro area alone had three. Everything cost more, including toll calls, phone installation, pizza slices, and meals at Arby's.

People seemed busy, less patient. The counter workers in restaurants weren't friendly local folk happy to chat, but hostile teenagers who wished they had better jobs or weary older people waiting for their shifts to end. If he or Eric hesitated at Dunkin' Donuts, the clerk simply turned to the next person in line. This kind of hostility bewildered them; they saw it not as an inevitable part of urban life, but as something personal and hurtful.

Eric said he missed the sun. He never seemed to see the sun in Chicago. Either it wasn't out, or it was obscured by buildings.

I'd brought Jesse some coffee and a doughnut, which he accepted without comment. He rarely ate breakfast, but I figured he might need some extra nourishment. Walking across the train station's vast parking lot, he seemed oblivious to the stream of grim, paunchy commuters on their way into the city. When I saw the map I realized with a jolt that Richton Park was the next-to-last stop on the Chicago Metra. Jesse was as close to Gary, Indiana, as he was to Chicago.

Learning that we were early, we walked the two blocks to Dunkin' Donuts and Jesse ordered black coffee and another glazed doughnut, took one bite, then threw the rest away. "My stomach is a little tight," he said. He looked terrified.

When I'd first met Jesse, I jotted the words "internal, anxious" in a notebook and underlined them three times, my signal that they were important. I thought that Jesse was one of the most guarded people I'd ever met. He weighed every word, especially those that had to do with the way he felt about things.

He seemed to experience a near-catatonia when confronted by circumstances that yanked him out of his familiar geek existence and into alien environments. I'd occasionally seen him turn so ghostly pale I thought he'd faint.

I wrote "brave" in one of those first notebooks too, because I realized that this wasn't a person for whom change came easily, even though he was about to undertake a world of it.

He took the coffee for the train, on the walk back ruminating about the nature of work in downtown Chicago. "I guess you work in those towers, in one of those cubicles. Cubicleville." He didn't like the idea. Emco Computer may not have been IBM, but you could relax there, move around, get online and game when things weren't busy, walk out to get a soda, work irregular hours as long as you got the job done. He enjoyed riding there on his bike. He could see he wouldn't enjoy the packed, rattling train. Most of his notions about corporate and office work came from reading *Dilbert*. From the few job inquiries he'd made, he already sensed that jobs in those towers would be different, much more structured, formal, and confining. He doubted you could game during work hours, or scarf new software from the Web, "burn" a friend's CD, or go on ICQ chat lines and trade funny commercials with friends you'd never met.

"The density," he kept saying. "The density."

Working in a giant tower with hundreds of people was almost

beyond his imagination. Making all that small talk with strangers. And what did he really know about this particular office? Was it a geek-friendly place? Could you wear sneakers? Were you surrounded by suits, like these people streaming toward the train?

Richton Park was nearly as grim as Caldwell, if a bit more middle-class and a lot more congested. It had almost the same dispiritingly drab quality and the same bottom line: an inhospitable place for a bright young kid with no friends to be living.

Spotting the computerized Metra card system, Jesse broke into a complex riff about magnetic codes—how they work, how hard they are to duplicate—which led to a long discourse on bar codes, which are, he said, easy to duplicate. In fact, he'd spent many happy hours on bar code websites where geeks gathered to compare, discuss, and trade codes and information. Some kids even printed out cheap bar codes and pasted them over the codes on more expensive products. It sometimes worked at superstores and giant chains where bored teenaged employees barely paid attention. "But magnetic codes," he sighed, "those are impossible." He didn't answer when I asked whether he considered train tickets material or intellectual property.

By 7:15, we were on the Metra, a huge double-decker commuter train headed downtown. It was a long, mostly grim trip past ugly suburbs, decaying industrial plants, slums, and vast rail and truckyards. The cars filled up with commuters silently sipping coffee or staring dully out the window. As we ran through a mini-rehearsal, I peppered Jesse with a few likely questions: What did he want to do in five years? How long had he been working with computers? How did he get along with peers?

We had a small wrangle about whether or not he needed to disclose his misdemeanor arrest record for driving under the influence. Absolutely, I said. It's none of their business, he countered. But if you don't, I argued, they might run some check on you and come up with it themselves. Then they can fire you. He'd sue, he huffed. One thing he'd learned in Idaho was to be suspicious of all this record-keeping; it was an invasion of privacy. Jesse was nearly indefinable politically, but libertarian probably came closest. There was almost no part of government he liked or trusted. "But you're building the world that makes it possible to get all this information," I couldn't resist needling. He conceded this was a valid point.

Two stops later, he decided he would tell them about the arrest. He also decided to call up Ryder and complain about the rental truck. "You can usually get them to give you a refund if you make enough noise." It wouldn't be a lot of money, maybe $60 or $75. Still, that would mean two weeks' food. The transmission was off, he said. The steering wheel rattled.

He remained undecided about the tie, his usually iron-clad geek philosophy failing him. This had nothing to do with fashion or style; it was a political issue that went to the heart of his identity, something he'd never compromised about. "If it's not a geek-friendly place, I don't want to be there," he explained. "I'll call Sherry and ask her to find something else. That's not why I moved all the way from Idaho, to be a suit working for suits. I couldn't survive it."

In Idaho, Jesse hadn't even owned a tie. But the night before he left, his mother, visiting from Montana to say good-bye, took him to JCPenney and bought him a Grateful Dead tie and some brown work shoes. Just in case. But Jesse realized last night that he didn't know how to knot a tie; moreover, he'd forgotten to pack the shoes, which was why Eric's borrowed pair were in his backpack. He'd used AltaVista to find a fashion site with necktie instructions, but he wasn't sure he'd gotten it right. I said I could show him.

Rummaging through his backpack, he discovered that he'd left behind the slip of paper containing the name of his interviewer and the company's exact address. He then proceeded to spill coffee over his pants leg. A woman across the aisle handed him a cup of water, which he poured over the stain. "Jeez, that's impressive," he muttered. "Showing up with a coffee stain on your leg." Maybe, since he was wearing brownish pants, it wouldn't show.

"I've never had a real job interview," he announced. Ernie, who'd hired him at Emco, hadn't asked him much beyond when he could start. Certainly he hadn't needed to dress up. He decided that the tie might present a safety issue. If pressed, "I can tell them that ties get caught in computer workings and can damage the computer or catch fire." It was, he insisted, remotely possible.

Desperate as he was for a job, he was determined not to sell out, not to "start on that road," as he put it. It was an interesting point of view for somebody a year out of high school who'd only had one job (except for summers at a skeet-shooting range outside Caldwell, where he dodged the wayward blasts of drunken, late-night shooters). It would be smart to put the tie on, he knew, and appear sober and respectable. Yet having appeared in a tie, would it become expected ever after?

He was clinging to his optimism despite neckwear inexperience and coffee stains. "I've done everything with computers," he reminded himself. "I've solved almost every conceivable kind of problem. I've built them, taken them apart, fixed them, installed software, written programs, installed and fixed modems, fixed hard drives, put in memory chips. I can't imagine there's too much they would need to know that I can't answer."

The train pulled into Hyde Park, which I remembered was the home of the University of Chicago and also where Clarence Darrow, the famous criminal attorney whose life had obsessed me when I was a kid, lived with his wife, Ruby. Looking out the train windows, we could see the university's Gothic spires. Five or six students got on, several reading books even as they walked down the aisles. One wore a stud in her lip, another was a self-styled Paris intellectual—beret, scarf tossed around the neck, volume of poetry.

Jesse took them in silently. He'd love to see what a real college campus looked like, he said; I mentioned to him that a kid from my town in New Jersey was in her third year there, loving it. She was awfully nice. Would he like to call her and maybe get a tour?

"God, I'd love that."

Don't you ever want to go to college? I asked, not for the first time.

"Sure," he said, "but it's not in the cards. No money, no time.

I don't have the grades either." He looked so mournful that I regretted having brought it up.

"I knew a kid in Idaho," he recalled as we resumed the journey toward the Loop. "His parents sent him to college, paid for the whole thing, tuition, room, and board." He snaps his fingers. "Just like that!" The idea seemed so astonishing to him that he pondered it silently for a minute or two.

Trying to keep his job-interview terror at bay, I asked about jobs he'd like. "My dream job? Working for the *National Enquirer*, doing computer graphics, you know, putting somebody else's body with Hillary Clinton's head." He added, more wistfully, that what he'd really like was to be a chemist or biologist.

After an hour's ride, the train pulled into Chicago. AltaVista had prepared Jesse well for this part of the trip; he sprinted up the stairs and through the station tunnels, emerged onto the street, turned left toward State Street, then north to Madison. He'd remembered the address, it turned out. But when he tried to call Sherry to get his interviewer's name, there was no answer. It was too early.

He called Eric, hoping he could locate the slip, but Eric didn't pick up; probably he was still asleep. Growing frantic, he plunked quarters into a phone booth in the lobby, called Eric again, then Sherry. He drifted across the street to another Dunkin' Donuts, but his stomach was still too queasy even for a glazed doughnut.

Sitting in a booth, we went over the interview questions one more time. "This isn't the only job," I assured him. "It's the first job interview. If nothing else, it will be good practice." But I could almost hear him mentally running through his spreadsheet. When we got up a few minutes later, I saw the sweat stains under his arms.

A traffic cop's whistle was shrieking at the intersection as we crossed back to the building. Cabs honked and the sidewalks were thronged with more people than pass through Caldwell in a year. "I don't see any kids my age," Jesse said, forlornly. Wherever he went, there were no kids his age.

He remembered that he had to change shoes and retreated to a corner of the lobby, out of sight of receptionists and guards, to sit on the floor and pull on Eric's brown Oxfords. I kept pumping quarters into the pay phone trying to reach Sherry. As a few office workers stared, Jesse stuffed his Airwalks into the backpack.

He would put his tie on after all, he decided. "I figure it's respectful to wear a tie during an interview, even if you decide later that you don't want to." Then he changed his mind.

He tried calling Eric and the broker again. Still no luck.

Fifteen minutes to go. He decided to take the elevator up and ask the receptionist for the name of the person who'd be interviewing him. He put on the tie, but needed help knotting it properly. And he promised to check out the office carefully to make sure there were geeks working without ties and jackets.

Two hours later, drained and distracted, looking almost about to pass out, Jesse descended. It took several minutes before he could talk easily.

It went well, he thought. The head of the Information Services unit had asked him to replace a hard drive. The other two interviewers had asked a bunch of questions about how he'd handle various repairs of the company's numberless desktops.

None of the questions threw him. He did, in fact, see a number of tie-less employees, and was reassured by one of his interviewers that nobody in his department would make an issue of neckwear.

There were still a couple of other people to interview, they told Jesse, but he was a leading candidate. "I had a good feeling about it," he said. Nevertheless, he still looked exhausted, even paler than normal. I bought him lunch, then he headed home, went back online, and began playing Quake II with Eric to wind down.

The day had completely emptied him as if, between my questions and the job interview, he had used up his entire reservoir of chatter, energy, and social grace. He lost himself online, in his character, in the search for weapons, in the running techno-patter with Eric about speed, graphics, power. He didn't speak again for three hours.

Two days later, Sherry called to tell Jesse he had the job. His starting salary as a support tech was far higher than his father's as a fire inspector in Idaho.

Three tense weeks after that, Eric took a temp job, as a network programmer with Andersen Consulting that paid $35,000 a year. After three months, he was told, the prospects of a permanent spot were very good.

Within a month, Jesse and Eric found a local Internet service provider and bought themselves a celebratory Nintendo 64.

There were some glitches. Jesse had assumed that phone rates worked the way they did in Idaho, that there was no charge for going online. The first $1,100 phone bill taught him the hard way that he was mistaken: The dial-in number was a toll call, unless you subscribed to a $100 plan that capped the costs. Eric nearly collapsed, and Jesse mustered all his well-honed phone skills with the telephone company, talking his way past the first rank to a supervisor, then claiming he was misled. The supervisor agreed to let him sign up for the special plan retroactively. Since they could never have paid the bill—and worse, couldn't have gone online—both were immensely relieved.

The incident revealed a pair of explorers still finding their way on the strange urban frontier. Jesse steeled himself and attended a coworker's Halloween party in a hip neighborhood, bolted when he felt utterly out of place, then spent the night websurfing at his office because the last train to Richton Park had already left. Then Eric's hard drive got wrecked during a thunderstorm, when rain poured in on it through an open window. Both were staggered by their long commutes.

But something essential, even profound, had changed. They'd gotten out of Caldwell. They'd made it to Chicago. They were employed.

And of course, something essential hadn't changed. Their nonworking lives completely revolved around the Net, trading MP3s, finding software, getting their hands on new games, trying out new operating systems. Weekends consisted of sleep, Web surfing, shopping for random groceries and fast food, perhaps catching a part of a movie. Neither had made new friends or met a girl. They were still together in their aloneness.

GEEK VOICES

August 1998

I guess the proudest thing about being a geek is that we start out tending to be behind, physically, socially, and experientially but we *improve.* We are the ones who are not satisfied with a nine-to-five job (don't ask how many things I work on besides my day job), not satisfied with Club Med vacations or Red Lobster cuisine (what percentage of techies are vegetarian these days?), not satisfied with ourselves. We improve whenever and however we can. At least from my experiences, at fourteen, my friends were pretty undistinguished in many ways, but I look around and we've ended up with clearer goals, better ethics, and fuller lives than the more conventional folks around us. The money hasn't hurt either. :)

—Rustin

From: Jesse Dailey
To: Jon Katz

Okay, so I'm sitting on the train and I fire up my portable intending to spend a nice intensely focused time installing and playing with Visual J++6 on my slow beast of a laptop. Across from me sit these two kids who are about ten or so . . . maybe 11 or 12 but not very old. So one of them pulls out his pocket Gameboy and starts to play while the other watches and both continue to argue about what character is better. . . .

Eventually the argument reaches a fervent pitch and the friend pulls out his pocket Gameboy and his 3 port networking cable. They proceed to hook up right there and fight it out to settle once and for all who is better . . . when one of them wins the other one says, "Okay, who do you want?" and the loser is forced to download one of his characters over to the winner's machine. They were fighting for pink slips on role playing characters.

This is the kind of stuff I would have killed to do when I was ten years old. . . . These kids have computers at home they

were talking about also, and in 5 years they are gonna be
doing things that haven't even been introduced to us yet, and
then in 10 they'll be doing it in a way better than we ever will
be. These guys were geeks in training and as soon as they realize it they are gonna kick the pants off of me.

> > >

THE PLAN for the first Thanksgiving either Jesse or Eric had
ever spent away from their families was to order a pizza, then
turn to the important stuff: Quake and Half-Life, an advanced
new computer game they'd borrowed and copied—"burned"—
with very cool blood-soaked graphics. In fact, Jesse announced,
he thought it was time I had my first computer game "kill." I
overheard him whispering to Eric, asking if he'd disabled the
kill functions of the other players.

I'd watched Jesse and Eric play for hours; I knew I wouldn't
last three seconds before some strange creature popped up out
of a hallway and blasted me to bits. Jesse practically melded
into the computer casing when he played, his entire neural system wired into his character. He was completely focused and
alert, firing a stream of laser bursts, anticipating enemies, collecting armor and medicine. I was too old to summon those
kinds of reflexes.

Sure enough, when I took the controls, a dozen commandos
jumped out and blasted away. Miraculously, nobody hit me. I
fired back and one grunted and dropped to the ground.

"Hey, congratulations," Jesse beamed. A new kind of ritual
initiation; I found myself curiously proud despite the fix being
in. Then Jesse and Eric took over.

They wondered if their parents would call. (They didn't.) They wondered which takeout place would deliver a plain cheese pizza on Thanksgiving Day. AltaVista provided the answer: Aurelio's.

But then, for no discernible reason, Jesse decided that pizza lacked panache. They should cook their first dinner in Illinois, a proper one, to mark the occasion. So they headed out to walk the three blocks to the Eagle Country Market.

The place was quiet, nearly deserted but for some last-minute shoppers—almost all middle-aged women—scrambling for an odd or end to complete Thanksgiving dinner. Except for the cashiers, Jesse and Eric were the youngest people in the market by twenty years.

Soon they were huddled at the end of the first aisle, in the unaccustomed position of pushing a shopping cart. Did they want frozen turkey? Corn? Gravy? They grabbed a six-pack of lite beer, then got bogged down in the instant potato section.

"Look, these are Idaho spuds," Jesse called out, picking up a package. He and Eric always looked to see if potatoes were from Idaho, one of the few manifestations of loyalty to their home state.

"Those are awful," warned a woman passing with a cart. They regrouped, comparing five or six varieties to study the microwave time: anything that required longer than four or five minutes was unfeasible, given that every course had to wait its turn in their small countertop oven.

They finally settled on a mix with herbs, two packages of frozen ON-COR turkey, also microwaveable; a can of gravy; a package of frozen corn; some stuffing mix that could be boiled with water if they could locate a pot; a $3.99 frozen pecan pie and some Reddi-Wip. The bill came to $37.35.

Back at the Cave 2.0, they cooked Thanksgiving dinner in their own particular way, passing back and forth between the kitchen and their computers, wordlessly sticking turkey slices in the microwave while glancing at the football game on TV, playing Half-Life, or asking something of AltaVista. Eric killed a few aliens while Jesse prepared the stuffing.

Eric picked up a book he'd ordered online, *How to Succeed with Women,* by Ron Louis and David Copeland, and read aloud from a chapter called "The Seven Habits of Highly Effective Seducers," which prompted an argument about whether it was okay to grovel for sex. (Jesse and Eric never thought it was okay to grovel for anything.)

Not that the issue had arisen yet. Their social adventures had been mixed, but familiar. Eric wouldn't be invited to his company's holiday party because he wasn't a full-time employee yet. Jesse went to the Chicago Film Festival where he met a friendly and attractive Finn, but she barely spoke English. Both were invited to a rollerdome on the South Side where, to their mutual horror, they found themselves at Gospel Roller-skating Night, complete with pauses for prayer.

The reality was that though people had been kind enough to include them in events, they remained very much apart. Eric missed having even the few friends they had in Idaho, who'd come over to play games and browse the Web.

"The really hard thing, but something I guess I'm used to,"

Jesse reflected, "is that we're still out of sync. I'm the youngest person in my office. People my age are in college, mostly, or in different kinds of jobs. I'm too young to drink, so I can't go out with everybody to bars after work, which is what they do." It's different, he said, and yet the same.

Still, by the end of the year, Eric would be making nearly $40,000 and Jesse about the same—several times their income in Idaho just a few months earlier. And both were working for big companies with lots of benefits and possibilities. They could even afford Coca-Cola instead of their customary generic pop, and brand-name Kraft macaroni and cheese; this was a source of distinct pride.

Their biggest regret?

"Moving to a town with no cable modem access," Jesse reported sadly. "So we are slow on the Web." According to AltaVista, source of all knowledge, though surrounding suburbs were wired, no service was even planned for Richton Park. They were talking about a move as soon as there was enough money.

Meanwhile, downloading software and MP3s was sometimes agonizingly slow; even worse, they'd gotten their butts kicked when they went online to play Quake or Half-Life against geeks who did have cable modems. "No way you can move fast enough to keep from getting killed against somebody with cable access," Eric lamented.

As in Idaho, they'd worked themselves into a kind of routine, bounded by age, social realities, money, and the Net. Fearless online, cautious socially. Fast-food meals, though Jesse had dis-

covered Thai takeout downtown. Almost no new furniture, two
bedrooms turned into the familiar shambles of clothes and
books, not the slightest domestic touch in the apartment. A
phone with Caller ID, best friend of the occasionally delin-
quent bill payer. Long days of work and commuting, evenings
online.

Apart from movies, weekends were constructed around
some new Net or Web project—trying out a just-purchased
game, downloading new software, collecting and listening to
music, installing a new operating system. There was no end to
this incessant exploring, finding new sites, going on ICQ and
Hotline Connect to trade or play chess. The Net filled in all the
blanks in their lives.

There was a problem with the turkey—not enough time to
nuke both packages—but one would serve. It was dinnertime.
The table, usually reserved for CDs and programming manu-
als, was cleared and was as close as it would ever get to groan-
ing, with a plate of turkey slabs, a bowl filled with instant herbal
mashed potatoes, some microwaved corn, and boiled stuffing.
And real Coke.

"Not too shabby," Jesse said, surveying it all. "Our first meal."
Eric took out the paper plates they used on the rare occasions
they didn't get fast food, but Jesse suddenly balked. "Heck, this
is Thanksgiving," he said. "Let's use real plates."

"Do we have three plates?" Eric wondered. Rummaging
around in some lower shelves, they dug out several, filled them
with food, then sat on the floor between the computer and the
TV. In their own way, both were formal, gracious. Eric wondered

if they should say something. "Thanks," Jesse intoned. "Thanks for getting us out of Idaho." Eric nodded and they dug in.

Through the door of Jesse's bedroom, hanging on a closet door knob, was the corduroy porkpie he used to wear to Middleton High. He hadn't worn it much since, but it was one of the few things he'd kept and brought to Chicago.

Afterward, Jesse leaned back in their only armchair, stuffed and satisfied, in a rare moment away from the TV or computer screen. Always wary of tempting fate, or sounding "prideful," Jesse refused to gloat about having pulled off this move. But they had, in fact, come halfway across America on their own wits and meager resources. They'd started up the ladder of upward mobility. They'd joined the geek technocracy.

And they insisted they weren't going back. Jesse was right: It *was* easier to strike out alone than to try to fit in. They were on their own, still searching in this new place for compatriots and allies.

Jesse raised his glass of Coke in a toast. "Here's to the community of social discontents," he said.

From: Jesse Dailey
To: Jon Katz

So, with much regret I'm backing out of the company Christmas party. I just don't have any kind of right attire to go. It's business attire, like jacket required. This is something I really wanna go to . . . for networking reasons and just for personal exposure to fellow human beings who would be mostly friendly. I may not fit tightly or very well with them yet, but it could be fun, and the whole damn company is going to be there. I feel like I'd really be missing out.

I may stop by the super cheap suit store on the way out of here, and see if maybe I can pick something up for not too much money that I could at least wear once.

GEEK VOICES

July 1998

I've a fair amount of war wounds from suits—I used to work at a bank. Geekdom, at least for me, is not something I usually think about and is only incidental to a far larger, more important thing: I am, first and foremost, unequivocally, an individual. I want my gravestone to read, "Thinker, creator, lover, freak."

—Brian (if you get bored,
feel free to check out
my links page . . .)

From: Jon Katz
To: Jesse Dailey

Jesse, would you describe your life as having been painful?

From: Jesse Dailey
To: Jon Katz

I don't know how to answer. I don't have the words. The best answer is for you to go to Chapter Sixteen of David Copperfield. You'll know the part when you see it. That's how I feel about myself. I can't say it any better.

> > >

IF YOU'RE going to ask somebody to speak for you, I e-mailed back, it might as well be Dickens.

I did know the passage when I saw it:

It seemed to me so long, however, since I had been among such boys, or among any companions of my own age . . . that

I felt as strange as ever I have done in all my life. I was so conscious of having passed through scenes of which they could
have no knowledge, and of having acquired experiences foreign to my age, appearance, and condition as one of them,
that I half believed it was an imposture to come there as an
ordinary little school-boy. I had become . . . so unused to the
sports and games of boys, that I knew I was awkward and in-
experienced in the commonest things belonging to them.
Whatever I had learnt, had so slipped away from me in the
sordid cares of my life from day to night, that now, when I
was examined about what I knew, I knew nothing.

A computer geek who explains himself through Dickens is
less remarkable a phenomenon than one might think. Geeks'
passions often crisscross back and forth between technology
and more traditional forms of culture, with unusual depths of
interest in both. One programmer I know loves Disney animation; another calls himself a "hardware and sailing geek." An
e-mail correspondent has memorized the script of every *Simpsons* episode. I've encountered a geek with newly minted coins
from around the world and one who's written an elaborate digital music script for all of Beethoven's works.

At Jesse's suggestion, I visited a giant bar code site where
geeks gathered on weekends to talk about bar code technology.
Yet Jesse had also picked up *David Copperfield* from a discount
bin at the Waldenbooks near his office, and it had rocked him.

Jesse and Eric were thankful for their deliverance, but it was
shocking, even disheartening, to see that while they'd ridden
the Internet halfway across the country, in some ways they
hadn't gone anywhere.

Outside their apartment, almost everything about their lives was different. Inside, almost nothing was.

The same computers sat on the same tables, surrounded by the same ratty chairs and lampless rooms with bare walls. The nearly empty refrigerator held the same packets of Chinese takeout sauce, even the same Katz Diet Coke can, which I'd bought in Idaho and they'd carefully transported across the Great Plains. The same clothes were strewn on the uncarpeted floors.

They were living almost exactly as they had in Caldwell. There was work, sleep, and a life shaped around computing, technology, and the Net.

Although they'd never mentioned it, I'd been startled to see that almost everyone else living in the Richton Park apartment complex was black. They didn't seem to notice or even slightly care, but though Jesse shared many geeks' Net-spawned tolerance (since you never know anyone's race, sexual orientation, or even, sometimes, gender online, they just don't matter much), the racial and cultural differences made a social life even less likely. The residents were not only overwhelmingly African American, but generally considerably older.

One night, Jesse had spotted a young guy he suspected might be a geek on the train, but he never saw him again. Other than that ephemeral close encounter, he hadn't had a single interaction with another human in Richton Park in the three months he'd lived there.

Work was proving tricky to maneuver, too. After his initial terror eased, the tasks had quickly become routine, yet the environment felt strange. Jesse had a rough time figuring out his

boss's expectations. One coworker was openly hostile and competitive, the first time Jesse had ever encountered office politics. He couldn't believe how much like "Dilbert" work really
was, he told me over and over. There were meetings, which
made him feel boxed in and claustrophobic. Eric, too, was
shocked by the bureaucracy and politics surrounding his job,
and bristled at the temporary help-desk work he was assigned
(answering phone calls for technical assistance)—the bottom
rung of the geek pecking order.

Jesse's company also frowned on Net explorations during
work hours, and installed filtering software to keep employees
off porn and other recreational sites, so Jesse had to be careful
when he trawled the Net or burned or downloaded music.

Geeks keep their computers on round-the-clock and often
work irregular hours, in part because Web-surfing, software
trading, and collecting and ICQ and Hotline messaging are fac-
tored in. Geek-friendly companies tolerate, even encourage
this: The more wired and current geek employees are, the
quicker they are to spot bugs and glitches, the better and more
efficiently they can set up operating and security systems, run
up the best spreadsheets and database programs.

At companies run by suits, such activities definitely don't
qualify as work. Straight companies are also paranoid about
employees getting into pornographic websites or downloading
violent games, let alone pirated CDs, software, and movies.

It felt a bit like school, the first time in a while that Jesse had
to hide his geek activities. Ernie had never cared what Jesse or
other Emco techs did online as long as they got their repairs

done. Now Jesse's supervisors wanted him to appear absorbed in something conventional, even when he had nothing to do.

Meanwhile, there was Chicago.

Jesse was still talking about the man he'd seen a few weeks back, dressed as Jesus—robe, wooden cross and all. He'd walked into a downtown restaurant where Jesse was eating, took an adjacent table, and politely ordered dinner.

An urbanite now, Jesse browsed discount book stores. He'd walked past his first gay bar, encountered his first drag queens. He bought some slightly hipper shirts and shoes. Chinese take-out replaced Taco Bell as his lunch of choice. He made a couple of friends at work, people who were older but with whom he could occasionally go out to lunch.

STILL, THE ability of these two to instantly pick up the digital rhythms of their lives and make them focal points of their existence was striking, and sometimes disturbing. Their entrenched inwardness, a profoundly interior consciousness, seemed at times woven into their personalities.

I called Jesse up one day to tell him the president had been impeached. He was stunned. "You're kidding!" He and Eric went on CNN.com to read about the House of Representatives' vote and even discussed it for an hour or two. Then he never mentioned it again. For geeks, both politics and journalism represent—in Jesse's words—"an insane and useless" system that has little bearing on their lives.

Making computers work requires a particularly rational mind. Programming, the installation of software, getting computers to speak properly to one another, all require very particular languages, protocols, and conventions—in sharp contrast to the emotional, visceral, manipulative drama of the political system. Jesse could hardly comprehend a Congress that would care about a president's sex life. Or one that passed a Communications Decency Act to ban dirty language on the Internet.

He actually refused to believe me when, some months later, I informed him that the House had passed a bill allowing public schools to post the Ten Commandments. Why should he pay the slightest attention to a system like that? Where did these people get the gall? He wasn't inclined to fight it or change it, he simply had nothing to do with it, blocked it out. He didn't know who the mayor of Chicago or the governor of Illinois was, nor did he care.

He saw himself as a citizen of the Net, a separate nation with rules, boundaries, and traditions of its own. He was free to go where he pleased, take what he wanted. Other than paying for bandwidth, which he bitterly resented, he was subject to no regulation, no taxes, no restrictions on his ability to say what he wished.

Such citizenship had certain lingering limitations. One weekend a few months after he'd moved, I heard on my car radio that a vicious blizzard had hit Chicago, closing the airports, shutting down public transit, stranding cars on highways. Mindful of his father's warning that if anything would send Jesse packing for Idaho, it would be Chicago's winters, I called that afternoon to ask the boys about their first big snowstorm.

Jesse was shocked. He and Eric had been engrossed in some complicated networking program all morning and were about to go catch the Metra downtown in search of a theater—as usual, they didn't know which movie or what theater at what time.

"But I hear there's a blizzard in Chicago," I said. "In fact, I'm watching it on CNN." The storm was impressive, overwhelming snow-clearance efforts; the mayor had declared a state of emergency.

There was a pause, while I heard Jesse yell to Eric, "Hey, man, look outside. It's really snowing out there." Eric was dispatched to peer out the window at the train station across the street. He reported that the tracks were snow-covered and that the trains didn't seem to be operating.

"Good thing you mentioned this," Jesse said. "I guess I was aware that it was snowing, but I just hadn't paid much attention."

Would anything, I wondered, ever seem more compelling to them than the Internet? The two always were neck-deep in a techno-project, but only sporadically conscious of the world around them. Their already substantial computer knowledge was growing daily—they were keeping pace with every advance or evolution of the Net and the Web. But they weren't making parallel progress in their personal lives.

I was sorry I hadn't spoken up more forcefully about the risks of apartment hunting via search engines. Journalistic detachment was one thing, letting kids walk blindly into a trap was another. Jesse couldn't have found a less appropriate community if he'd asked AltaVista: "What's the worst place in the greater Chicago metropolitan area for two nineteen-year-old kids from Idaho to live?"

Once the novelty of moving wore off, I feared Jesse would sink into the same torpid, depressed state he'd been in back in Idaho, only worse. He was stuck in a grim Chicago suburb almost as far from an interesting cultural life as Caldwell was. Only he had a non-geeky office job and a long commute to endure as well. Because Chicago's clubs, museums, music, and theater were distant, and Jesse and Eric were so dependent on the Metra train, they went out rarely. He'd even lost his only source of physical exercise now that distances were too far to bike and the weather too bitter and snowy. They lived a surreal, quasi-adult existence, becoming sober straphangers as many of their peers were getting drunk at frat parties.

Sure enough, the crash came that winter. "I'm glad we left Idaho," Jesse told me one night on the phone. "But I admit it, this is a letdown. Long commute, dull job, no social life." I reminded him that he wasn't stuck: He could move, switch jobs, consider college. He was nineteen. He didn't have to stay mired in a Richton Park rut any more than he'd been doomed to one in Idaho.

This message always did the trick with Jesse. His life had consisted of a series of traps and obstacles—all the way back to the Nampa gang—that he'd slip or bump into and come to see as his inevitable fate. But once reminded that he could get out, he usually did. He loved making plans, solving problems. He began sniffing around for jobs and other apartments.

The one area where no amount of prodding seemed to work was his social skills. He hadn't met anyone his age. Sometimes it seemed to me he just didn't have the strength. One woman at work had invited him to lunch a couple of times, but since she

didn't know or care much about computers, he wasn't inter-
ested. Nor did the isolation seem to bother him, particularly.
He reminded me that they hadn't known their neighbors in
Idaho either.

Although both Jesse and Eric professed to wanting marriage
and a family—Jesse clearly imagined himself a suburban dad
one day—that was well in the future, far away. For now, their
friendships were online, and their world was on a screen.

When I asked Eric about this, he verbally shrugged. "All I
know is I'm never going back to Idaho," he said. "I feel as if my
life has been saved." He'd always shown less interest than Jesse
in engaging with the broader world. He'd accomplished his first
great goal—moving—and hadn't yet focused on the next.

With Jesse, who agreed with my reservations about their so-
called new lives, I went many rounds. Our discussions and arguments sometimes ping-ponged from e-mail to late-night
phone chats and back again. I had no difficulty with e-mail—I
got tons every day—but it was a medium that made it too easy
for Jesse to evade or ignore my questions, or to parry with one-
liners. To get him to think and talk, you had to pry him off the
computer, which wasn't easy. But generally, once we got rolling,
he enjoyed the musings, and especially, the battles.

Richton Park, he countered, was a good transition to life in
Chicago. In his head, he was still adjusting to the move, and to
life in an office tower. "It's so much like Idaho it doesn't feel
strange," he explained. "I know I need to get out of here, but it's
served its purpose. It's safe and cheap. It's not a bad place to get
our bearings."

Though he was sometimes discouraged that everything in his

life hadn't changed, he saw that much had. He was especially conscious of that when he glanced behind him.

Jesse valued friends and he was a good one, not only to Eric, but to his pals back in Idaho, whose relationships and work lives were faltering one by one. Some were descending into depression, drugs, alcohol. Though he was now far away, Jesse e-mailed them constantly, even telephoned—a major step for him.

He continuously exhorted them to get out of Idaho, to not give up. Sometimes, I was interested to hear, he was telling them things I had told him months earlier: You can change the outcome; there are prospects and opportunities.

On one visit to Chicago, I met one of Jesse's oldest Idaho friends. Jesse had urged him to come visit, even sent him some money for the trip in the hopes that it might spark a similar impulse to get out of Middleton. Jesse's age, the friend was unemployed, had just fathered a kid and gotten divorced. He sat mutely for hours staring at the tube, playing video games; he seemed stoned or depressed almost beyond words. "I'm fucked up," he told me, each word coming slowly. "I'm an alcoholic, I guess."

I barely knew this kid, but I had no doubt he wasn't leaving Idaho anytime soon. Jesse couldn't believe how many of his friends were ending up like this. He could name the two or three who weren't.

But, he acknowledged, most of them weren't geeks. They didn't have the same odds. "They aren't part of any rising movement," he said. "They are headed for dead-end jobs in dead-end places. They can't even get into the army anymore." The modern army, smaller and increasingly high-tech, was getting quite choosy about its recruits.

I persisted, as always. What about a balanced life, one with room in it for more than work and the Net? He knew perfectly well what I was talking about, but didn't know what to think— or do—about it. I pushed, but didn't want to push too hard.

Jesse already carried a lot of burdens. He was the organizer of the pair, the bill-payer, the voice. He felt deeply responsible for Eric, who could be cheerfully upbeat but could also grow morose and withdrawn and sometimes would sink into deep funks, not talking for days. Jesse made it possible for him to function this way. Then he would come out of it, and the two would go out to dinner, then plunge into writing some program or into a long battle over which operating system was superior.

Despite that role, Jesse was more fragile than he let on, or would ever admit. Many things took more energy than he liked to acknowledge. It was obvious that he wanted a fuller life for himself, a girlfriend, more interesting work, a handful of loyal buddies to hang out with, cultural stimulation beyond snippets of movies.

But until he got that, the Net was his life and he wasn't about to let go of it. He had dug a hole for himself: He loved the Net and found it safe, so he spent almost all his free time there. Because he spent all of his free time there, he couldn't quite manage to broaden his life.

He wanted to, he said. He was already growing restless. "Part of my personality doesn't want to sit still. I can't stand to be in the same place for very long," he told me. "I'm totally sick of my job. I cannot stay in this place. I do expect more in the way of a social life. I do want it. I do care about it. It's bad . . . it's not nice to feel restless, to feel discontented. . . . I'd like to be content."

We both laughed. A part of Jesse knew he might never be content. "Maybe more content," he said.

"Getting here, getting to this place—this was all that I can do for now. I'm seeking technology as I always have, as more of a refuge, a place to hide. Technology for me—the Net and the Web—is a safe place to go, a safe thing to do."

But maybe, I suggested, technology was also keeping him from a broader life, preventing his getting out and doing the sometimes hard work that goes into building friendships and relationships. Maybe the Net provided too much cover.

Maybe, he allowed.

"It's a big fuzzy question," he said, struggling uncharacteristically to put the words together. "A social life is something I mean to have, have to have. I know it. I guess I can't do it until I'm ready, and it's taken everything I have just to get here. I guess I'll do it when I can."

JESSE COULD muster tremendous energy and enterprise once he got rolling, but he often needed a push. Our relationship had taken on this pattern: I gently prodded him to do something; he would mull it for days or weeks. Then, if he agreed—he often didn't—he'd take off like a rocket. Without knowing it or meaning to, I had jump-started his search for a life outside Idaho by telling him he could probably find a job anywhere.

So I started doing the same thing with some of the city's cultural offerings. Knowing the two still had little money to spare, I called a local ticket agency, ordered a couple of tickets to a local jazz club and to the Chicago Film Festival, and had them delivered to his office downtown. The trick, I realized, was not to talk about it. Jesse and Eric both had fierce pride about taking gifts or money; the way to help them was not to ask if you could.

Jesse never mentioned either event but, weeks or even months later, he or Eric would refer to the concert as an "awesome" experience or recall some "neat" film.

Eric was scrupulous about thanking me. He remained guarded and wary, especially about work and bosses, and he was never comfortable talking on the phone, but he was gracious, appreciative and, at times, surprisingly warm. "You're an angel," he e-mailed me one day abruptly. "Thanks for helping to get us out of Idaho."

Jesse almost never formally said thanks, but his gratitude was clear. And he often reciprocated. I'd begun writing for a new website, Slashdot.org, an intensely geeky techno/pop-culture site devoted to the open source Linux operating system and to the open source and free software movements. (This is a global geek political movement committed to building good software and distributing it for free, so that a handful of corporations won't dominate the Web the way they do the rest of the world.)

Mesmerized by the politics of open source, I'd started writing for the site for free. But my arrival was controversial, a bruising initiation. Most of the geeks who hung out on Slashdot had never come nose-to-nose with a professional writer on the

Web before, let alone one with few technical or computing skills. I was "flamed"—roasted by fierce criticism—within an inch of my life for months.

Jesse read every column I wrote, sending critiques, offering ideas. There was hardly a day that he didn't tip me off to some new website or evolving phenomenon like the rise of the MP3 online music movement. Without ever saying so, he was propping me up.

The idea of moving into the city had also been jump-started. Jesse and Eric both got promotions at work, and Jesse e-mailed me a new spreadsheet showing he'd need about $3,000—deposits for a new place, penalties to get out of the old, another truck, etc. He'd established a fund. It might take a year, he thought, but this time, he'd find a neighborhood with a better commute and—far more important—cable modem access.

And one more jump-start: In late winter, I sent Jesse the e-mail address of Jane Mahoney, a junior at the University of Chicago whom I knew from my town in New Jersey. She'd said she would be happy to show him around the school.

To my surprise, Jesse instantly accepted the invitation and went to visit her. Jane gave him an afternoon-long tour of the campus, the dorms and classrooms, the computing lab.

I'd e-mailed Jane a message of caution: Jesse might be shy or guarded around her or other college kids. She wrote back that I was nuts. "Are you kidding?" she asked. "He didn't stop talking from the second he showed up. He was great. He loved it here. I could easily see him going to the University of Chicago."

True enough, Jesse gushed about the school for days. He

loved meeting Jane, loved seeing the computer lab, loved the feeling of the campus and the people he'd met.

So much for his often-invoked wariness of middle-class yups, which seemed to have evaporated despite the certain presence of Chicago students in hundred-buck shoes. And what had become of all that social awkwardness? Not only did Jesse not see the school as an alien environment, he seemed to feel he'd come home.

I knew from my own daughter's college visits that kids either connected with a campus when they saw it, or didn't. It was sometimes impossible for parents to see what attracted them, but such gut responses were not to be ignored. I e-mailed Jesse a one-line query: "How'd you like it?"

From: Jesse Dailey
To: Jon Katz

Oh, it was so cool. It was awesome. . . . I felt just completely at home there. I loved everything about it. I can't imagine how you even go to a place like that. I understand this is not in the cards for me. No way I could afford it or get in. I feel like I have the brains but not the grades or resources to even try.

GEEK VOICES

Hi, Jon,

What is being a geek all about? Anarchy. Pure and simple. It's not throwing spherical bombs and wearing a cape and wide-brimmed hat and plotting to bring down the government. . . . It's the ultimate in anarchy, dragging Joe Normal into the fight by teaching him what Freedom is, and letting him infect his friends.

I work on a help desk for a big ISP and I get the greatest glee telling folks that what they read, what they do, can't be traced. . . . The more people that know this, the less the triumvirate of government, industry, and media can get away with what they do now. As Mr. and Mrs. Normal, and their strange kids take the power back. :)

—Ken

ESCAPE FROM RICHTON PARK

From: Jesse Dailey
To: Jon Katz

I was thinking today, as I have for several years now, about geekdom and this rise that you are writing about, and I realized a few of the fundamentals that lay the groundwork for such a movement.

The first is basic human greed and its close cousin, envy. When you live in Seattle or San Fran or Berkeley, someone sees a Jag driving down the street (read: luxury and wealth) . . . people automatically associate technology (and geekdom, just not consciously) with that type of money in those places. This flow of envy and thus, of power, is, for the first time in the history of geeks, flowing in the other direction . . . breaking what has been the status quo for many years. . . . The whole focus of the geek movement (please help me find a better word than movement) is to reverse this flow of power to the point of maximum benefit, and this hasn't happened yet. . . .

You asked me some messages ago why I thought of Idaho as hell. . . . I think that may have been a little strongly worded, perhaps I was fighting with a bout of geek dejection at the moment . . . but I think being able to see the rest of the world making these changes, changing toward much more geek-friendly environments and me not being able to participate or experience the benefits of my class was really upsetting, and possible cause for dubious slander. . . .

I have to apologize for the long e-mails. . . . I've been reading your mail in the mornings then stewing over questions and answers all day then finally getting home (it's 3:45 a.m. here now) to answer them, and by then I have lots to say. :)

> > >

IN FEBRUARY, a friend at work told Jesse about a two-bedroom apartment in Lakeview, a funky, artsy enclave north of downtown. This time, he actually went to take a look at the place, checked out the neighborhood, liked what he saw. Though their rent from Caldwell to Richton Park to Lakeview had increased—from $500 to $670 to a proposed $1,050, reflecting their socioeconomic elevation—he and Eric could afford it.

But there wasn't enough in his fund, yet, for moving expenses. A friend of mine, hearing regular bulletins of the Saga of Jesse and Eric, offered to send a check for $1,000. "I don't know about taking money," Jesse said, reluctantly.

Two things he'd brought with him from Idaho were fierce pride and a strong sense of independence. Anything resembling charity was anathema. But when you approached indirectly and occasionally, it was sometimes possible to help.

"It isn't from me," I said. "It's from a wealthy person who wants to help." For some reason, this was different. I emphasized that this anonymous donor had volunteered what was, to her, a small sum and that she wouldn't miss it. I mailed the check along with her note, explaining that someone had stepped in to help her at a crucial point when she was young, and that she wanted to repay the favor this way; he never said a thing about it. It made the move doable months earlier than would have otherwise been possible.

Jesse negotiated with the Cave 2.0 management to get out of his lease—leaving behind the deposit and a month's rent—rented a Ryder truck, called the phone company to get the all-important cable modem process rolling. Then he and Eric hauled everything they owned to Lakeview.

It was harder this time—their furnishings and wardrobes hadn't expanded, but their hardware had. There was a new computer to transport, webcams and zip drives, an additional monitor. They began packing on Saturday morning, loaded the truck in the middle of the night, and made three trips back and forth from Richton Park. Jesse called it one of the most exhausting nights of his life—they didn't sleep at all—but it meant paying for only one day's truck rental.

It was their second move in just a few months, and this time, Jesse and Eric were actually moving to the Chicago they'd thought they were heading for six months earlier. However much time they spent online, they'd inevitably be exposed to city life.

"Everything was instantly different," Jesse said afterward, thrilled. "The traffic, the people, the food, the buildings." Amazed by the scores of inexpensive ethnic restaurants, they left Taco Bell behind for good.

Lakeview was racially and culturally mixed, which Jesse particularly loved. "I think every day," he said, "that there are more different kinds of people on my block than I saw my whole life in Idaho. It's very cool." There were young people all around, although not as young as they were.

There were movie theaters within an easy cab ride, even walking distance. A bustling gay neighborhood crammed with clubs, restaurants, and shops lay a few blocks to the west, although neither Jesse nor Eric ventured there often. A Barnes & Noble bookstore was just down the street, along with a Starbucks and other cafés and diners. They could bike along the nearby lakefront (although the bikes were soon stolen from their second-story back porch).

There might even be time to enjoy it all, now that they had ten-minute commutes by bus as opposed to ninety-minute treks by train and on foot.

More significantly, their online life had been dramatically improved by cable modem access and their new equipment.

Yet, much as they professed to enjoy the stimulation and convenience of an urban neighborhood, they took relatively little advantage of it. To Jesse, the constant in his life was his geekhood; that was the root, the constant, the identity he toted with him no matter where he went.

Week by week, he worked on his computing—his lengthening MP3 playlist, expanded hard-drive power and memory, the cable modem and webcams. It took him all night to download the movie *Phantom Menace,* which he'd already seen in a theater. Why spend all that time downloading a movie playing all over Chicago? "It's the geek thing to do. I got all the episodes of Matt Groening's *Futurama,* too, and I'm working on *The Simpsons.*" Like most geeks, Jesse had turned his computer into a cultural entity. He collected and listened to music with it, used search engines to do everything from ordering an evening meal to resolving a technical dispute. Increasingly, geeks were amassing video. Large, high-resolution monitors and quality speakers were turning their computers into sophisticated cultural centers in much the same way TV sets had morphed into family entertainment units.

They still didn't know anybody in the new building, though. "Life in Lakeview hasn't changed us by any means," Jesse said with some pride. "We still live the way we have."

It was true, I saw on a visit in March, as I was heading back east after a book tour. This apartment was dingy in an urban, not suburban way. A few blocks from Lake Michigan, the three-story red brick building was grimy, the halls airless. The Cave 3.0 was older than the others, with wood floors and higher ceilings, so the place had an echo.

It looked abandoned, even though they'd just moved in. The computers occupied the usual place of honor in the center of the living room, with an array of tangled cables, boxes for hard drives and webcams spread across the floor. The Katz Diet Coke had moved to the new refrigerator.

The only visible change was the new equipment. It had taken the two of them months to cobble together parts gleaned from the Web, from rummage bins at computer and electronics stores, and from the carcasses of discarded rigs at work—but they had finally assembled a new computer to replace the one that had died in Richton Park during a thunderstorm when they'd gone out and left the windows open.

Now, said Jesse, they really felt as if they'd left Idaho behind. And somehow, in the process, he had recovered enough energy to begin talking more seriously about a subject that had been hovering for months, sometimes unmentioned but rarely far from my mind or, as it turned out, from Jesse's.

His visit with Jane Mahoney had triggered ideas about college. The more he browsed the University of Chicago catalogue online, the more classes he saw that he'd like to take, and the more boring his routinized office job seemed by comparison.

Jesse rarely gave much thought to his future, but when he did, he could move quickly. Once he'd grasped the notion that he could get a job anywhere, he bolted from Idaho in a matter of weeks. Once he got to Chicago, he grasped another elemental lesson: All geek jobs aren't alike.

There are countless geek employment prospects at help desks, in maintenance and tech support. But the creative challenge is much higher up the food chain—in computing labs, medical research, artificial intelligence, advanced programming for institutions like NASA, and Web design and development—all requiring higher education.

Without a degree, Jesse would likely remain in a cubicle in an office tower, fixing and maintaining the computers of people who didn't like them but needed them. If he were lucky, he might get to do some programming, set up some systems. Jesse didn't have to imagine this fate: Such people were all around him, ticked-off employees in their late thirties and forties, lots of them pleasant and adequately compensated, but few of them happy or stimulated. Was this what he'd come halfway across the country for?

He saw right away that he and Eric needed college degrees to avoid dead-end jobs in taller buildings. They now knew they could make decent livings and be comfortable; it wasn't enough.

We had been kicking the idea of college around, Jesse and Eric and I, ever since they'd settled into their jobs. Eric, by now a full-time employee at Andersen, thought he might like a computing school; the University of Illinois at Urbana-Champaign had a top-flight one.

Jesse, agreeing with me that he ought to start slow, had signed up in January for a programming course at DePaul University's downtown campus. In the back of my mind, I was thinking about DePaul as a possibility for him. Run by the Jesuits, it had a reputation for helping immigrant and working-class kids through the hurdles of college. Jesse would probably meet some kids like himself there.

So he'd registered, maneuvering his employer into paying most of the tuition, and went one evening a week. It was a simple class, teaching programming that Jesse had mastered years earlier. He made no friends; in fact, he barely mentioned the school once he'd enrolled. Although he eventually got an A in the course, I could tell he'd been uninspired and unimpressed. Maybe higher education wasn't such a great idea, I thought. Maybe this was my middle-class expectation, not his.

But now he started asking me about college. What was it

like? How much did it cost? How many classes did you have to take? Was there any financial aid? Did a school like the University of Chicago ever make exceptions? Offer special programs? When he talked about Chicago, it was in a completely different way than he discussed DePaul. DePaul was like medicine you're supposed to take. The University of Chicago had fired his imagination.

From: Jon Katz
To: Jesse Dailey

Jess, do I get the sense you're thinking about the University of Chicago?

From: Jesse Dailey
To: Jon Katz

You might say I'm at the fantasy stage. That's all. You think there's any way?

Was there any way? I told Jesse the big decision wasn't whether to apply to the University of Chicago, but whether or not to go to college. He should look at this as the beginning of a process. "You can definitely go to college," I assured him. "I have no doubt you're smart enough, and that we can find a good one to take you. Going after this particular one, though, is the toughest possible road. You should know that." It was probably a mistake, a red flag that would make Jesse more determined to try to butt his way into one of the more competitive schools in America.

In a funny way, Jesse's ignorance of the college process helped. Had he been able to see my daughter and her friends dealing with the same process, he might have avoided it altogether. But his myopia emboldened him. He didn't know how many upper-middle-class kids spent hundreds of dollars on SAT courses to try to boost their scores. He had never heard of the advisers-for-hire who managed kids' applications, edited their essays, helped them package themselves. He only knew that he was smart enough.

For all the bumps in all the roads, Jesse had an almost infectious self-confidence. He argued that he could match science, math, and computing skills with anybody. On some level, I think, he'd decided that if he couldn't go to a school like Chicago, then perhaps he ought not go at all.

My wife and friends were skeptical. The University of Chicago was tough to get into if you had top grades and tough to stay in, famous for its grueling workload. Even if he were accepted, Jesse might go into culture shock; Middleton High hadn't prepared him for this.

I dropped in to visit a college adviser I knew and told her about Jesse's background and qualifications. "DePaul would be perfect. This is what the Jesuits are known for. Or, if he didn't like it there, go for the University of Illinois," she counseled. "Northwestern would be a long shot, but a shot. Don't let him apply to Chicago. He'll get rejected and discouraged. Believe me, he hasn't got a chance."

She pulled a folder out of her file drawer and read me the transcript of a previous class officer and honor student: 1480 SATs, soccer team captain, enthusiastic letters from adoring teachers, awards for community service. "She got rejected there," the adviser said. It was like having a bucketful of ice water tossed in my face—unpleasant, but attention-getting.

"You're not doing him a favor by encouraging him to do something like this," she said more gently. "You have to help him be realistic. If you start lower, he has a better shot of getting in, going, and surviving."

I told him what the guidance counselor had said. The prospect was unrealistic, and he'd have trouble competing if he got in. It made so much more sense to aim lower. "It's almost impossible," I said.

I wasn't making even a dent in his position. He wanted to go for it. He knew it was a long shot, he told me during one of our marathon late-night phone sessions, but he wanted to try. He could use "a bit" of my assistance. It was, for Jesse, a cry for help. If I couldn't see how he'd get in, neither could I see how I could discourage him from trying.

In fact, I called the admissions office to ask if the school would still look at a kid's application three months after the deadline had passed. "Are you kidding?" the staffer said. "We're sending out acceptance letters soon."

ERIC WAS interested too, talking about applying to the University of Illinois. I'd made the same kind of exploratory phone calls on his behalf, hoping for a more encouraging response, but didn't get one. The school's computing school was one of the hottest in the country, the admissions counselor said, and Eric would be up against kids with outstanding grades and achievements.

Still, he made plans to travel to Urbana-Champaign after work one night for an admissions-office appointment and a look around. He bought a train ticket and made a motel reservation. Then he fell asleep on the train, overshot Urbana-Champaign and had to hire a cab in the middle of the night for $70 to make it back to his motel.

On the campus tour next morning, he fell in love with the computing school, alas. The admissions office was helpful but blunt. Eric should wait until the fall, when he'd officially be an Illinois resident and tuition would be far cheaper. He shouldn't apply directly to the computing school; he should enroll as a liberal arts undergraduate, and take some of the courses necessary to compete academically with the other computing applicants, then transfer.

"The problem," the counselor told me afterward, "is that most of the applicants have many more advanced courses in math, physics, and science than Eric does. What would we tell them?"

It was sound advice, but Eric was downcast at the idea that he was unqualified to apply directly to the computing program. "I realize what I'm up against," he said. "This is going to be rough." He'd love to work at a research facility one day, and he understood he needed more education to do that. But I worried that the delay would discourage him, that he wouldn't reapply. I also wondered how life would be for one of the lost boys if the other went off to school; they'd been inseparable for so long.

Eric downloaded the so-called common application from the university's website. He said he'd probably apply the following year, but he wasn't sure.

Jesse, on the other hand, decided to begin the process months late and see how tough it became before he made a final decision. He was testing the waters in his cautious way, beginning to apply without having formally decided to apply. He could put the brakes on at any time. He could return to DePaul in the fall and pick up where he'd left off.

He and I made a list of things he had to do if he decided to go on. High school transcripts to be requested and forwarded. Teacher references. Financial aid forms. Essays. Endless paperwork.

The application process was Jesse-style, prolonged, distracted, interrupted by technological projects. He forgot about the application fee. He was initially stymied by the essays, which he tried to fire off as irreverent, impulsive e-mail messages. Administrators in Middleton didn't return his phone calls. He left critical forms lying on the floor for days.

I couldn't see how this was going to happen in time for Jesse to join the class of 2003. The admissions office said to go ahead with the paperwork, though; it could always be used the following year.

So Jesse slogged on, still holding off on a final decision, understanding the long odds. A natural writer, he quickly grasped the difference between e-mail chat and the more formal and grammatical prose the school wanted, and labored over his essay. His punctuation began to improve, and he was careful to use his spell-checker, plus various online dictionaries and style guides.

Barely unpacked from Caldwell, his perpetual restlessness

was back with a vengeance. He could foresee a life of boredom and routine, not one of ideas and puzzles. And Jesse wasn't one to accept the cards dealt him.

He e-mailed me the "essay" he finally wrote, a poem modeled on one by Langston Hughes:

From: Jesse Dailey
To: Jon Katz

Instructions from the University of Chicago Office of Admissions:

Essay Option 1:

"The instructor said, Go home and write/ a page tonight. And let that page come out of you- Then, it will be true."
   The second line of this poem by Langston Hughes, "Theme for English B," goes on to ask: "I wonder if it's that simple?" We ask you here to write a truthful page about yourself, beginning where Hughes begins: "I am twenty-two, colored, born in Winston-Salem./I went to school there, then Durham, then here/to this college on the hill above Harlem./I am the only colored student in my class." That is to say, each of us is at a certain stage of life and has a history. Each of us has lived somewhere and gone to school. We each are what we feel and see and hear, as the poem goes on to say. Begin there and see what happens.

I am 20, white, a child of the working class.
I was born amid crazies devoted to Christ.
Of his name, though not of his words, did they preach.

Mother discovered transgressions past,
Sins of the man chosen to lead us.
And aside she was cast.
"Bad Spirits" they said.
"Bad Spirits" she had gathered.
"Bad Spirits" she would spread.
There followed divorce, and life thrown awry.
We left, outrunning the spirits.

Many years later, I landed back in the nest.
Come home to discover the changes of late.
Father with Parkinson's,
A new marriage completed,
Though hardly a new mother.
Spirits were not lost to her.
They were her solace, her peace.
She drank them the same way, and as quickly
As she drank the life out of my father,
Though still not nearly as quickly as disease.
A happy homecoming it wasn't.
I left, outrunning the spirits.

To a small apartment on the outskirts of a town
Stuck on the outskirts of the world.
Life here was tough, and for the first time
I began to appreciate my mother's masterful touch.
I learned about money, how it's never enough.
I learned about love, how there's never too much.
I saw for the first time the horizons of life, how they are
always too close.
For a 20-year-old, white child of the working class,
Those horizons were far closer than I like to admit.
The spirits had found me.

The change happened quickly,
A matter of moments.
I was sitting and thinking,
When suddenly it hit me:
I was free.
There is nothing to tie me down.
There is no one here to dictate my horizons.
I held in my hand the greatest gift I could have given myself.
The gift of freedom,
the gift of the future.

I had given myself a gift of the future,
And as I turned it around in my hand,
it felt a lot like a steering wheel.
A steering wheel attached to a
Sluggish yellow moving truck,
Plummeting eastward,
With reckless abandon,
Outrunning the spirits.

Jesse's grades, when the transcript arrived, were mediocre, far below what he seemed capable of. He tended to do well in math, science, and English, but even that record was spotty—he once got an F in a Shakespeare course. Teachers like Mr. Brown had spotted his intellect and tried to fan it, but others were annoyed by his wise-guy rebelliousness. There were few, apart from Mr. Brown, who would remember him fondly or go to bat for him, and he couldn't show much in the way of extracurricular activities or community service projects that demonstrated his potential.

He was a whiz at the state's Academic Decathlon, where he

competed in quiz show–style competitions and wrote essays on deadline. Still, it wasn't much to show one of the country's toughest schools.

Jesse's assets were obvious, but not easily documented, unless the admissions committee wanted to check out one of his pirated music sites and watch him scarf up downloaded CDs.

I was trying to be supportive and protective at the same time. Chicago and its students pride themselves on the university's intellectual rigor and demanding standards. In recent years, the administration has worked to lighten the load a bit, cultivate a less grim image, but I told Jesse that my daughter had heard the university referred to as "where fun goes to die."

Jesse laughed. "That's the place for me," he said.

My pessimism was heightened by watching my daughter and her friends go through this insanely intense process. She had the support and involvement of parents, teachers, friends, and an involved, knowledgeable college adviser at her high school. She'd been driven from one possible campus to another, visiting friends at schools she was interested in. Her transcripts were full of the advanced placement courses that admissions committees look for.

I tried to explain to Jesse how she had been groomed for college for much of her young life. There was never a question in her mind or ours, in the expectations of her teachers and classmates, that she would go. For years, she had understood what that would take, and had worked hard to get there.

But Jesse had never expected college, nor had anyone around him. He'd had no motive for working hard academically, and he was deeply distracted by personal and familial problems and in full-blown rebellion almost every day of his high school life.

Now he was two years older than his fellow applicants, was months late, had no money, and his family was very far away. Although he had little trouble getting As in classes he liked, he had a C+ average and his ACT test scores were below the mean at the university.

"Jeez, this is pretty unlikely, isn't it?" Jesse e-mailed me after reading a *Newsweek*-online story about how applications at the University of Chicago had jumped more than 30 percent in the past year. "Even if I did by some fluke get in, I couldn't pay for it." I urged him to keep an open mind, while quietly thinking he had a point.

"You don't have to tell me anything about low expectations," he said. His boredom grew, even though he was promoted again at work.

I'd supported, even instigated, the college talk, but I'd underestimated just how problematic getting him into college would be.

"The problem isn't that you're not smart," I said. "Everybody can see that. The problem is that you have to *show* them that you're smart—give them something to put in their folders, to put their hands on. The only way I can think to do that is for you to write something."

From the first, I'd been struck by Jesse's writing. Some of it was formal and trumped-up, overdone. Some of it was beautiful, powerful—as he would put it, "fiercely intelligent." He had that rare quality in any writer—a distinctive voice. I suggested he write a second essay, a letter to the dean of admissions that might anticipate his likely questions and reservations. He agreed to try.

His first drafts were always sketchy and abrupt like e-mail—and he resisted my editing suggestions—but he did listen when I badgered him to take more time, consider more carefully what he wanted to say. This was his attempt to explain himself.

Mon. May 10, 1999

Dear Dean O'Neill,

It occurs to me that the people who will be reading this letter are faced with a difficult decision concerning my admission to the University of Chicago. Namely, why would one of the country's most academically challenging universities accept me, an applicant whose GPA is probably lower than most, when so many better qualified candidates—at least on paper—have been turned away? Since I know that's what any admissions committee will most likely be asking, I'm writing to offer an answer.

My paper academic records are not a reflection of my intelligence or willingness to work. They are a reflection of my circumstances at the time.

The period during which these records were being forged was one of deep personal turmoil and pain for me, and for those who surrounded me.

My father had been diagnosed as having Parkinson's disease several years before. My mother was living far away in Montana. The disease had advanced very quickly, and had taken him to the point where he was nearly incapable of leading a normal life. He volunteered to be one of six people in the country to go under the knife for experimental brain surgery that would possibly provide him with a few more years of functionality. He has, unfortunately, steadily degraded over the last several years despite this augmentation of his brain functions.

There was a bitter divorce during the fall of my junior year. One more bit of wind added to the torrent.

At the same time, I was in the middle of a full-blown rebellion against almost all of the things I found around me in the world. I was trying to discover myself—and survive perhaps—by exploring the world in dangerous ways. All of it, not just the good part.

I started experimenting with drugs, and became involved with a gang in a nearby town. My attitude about the level of performance in school was altered for the worse, and dramatically so. I was challenging everything I knew and thought and was told. This may have been made easier for me because I was something of a social outcast, taking on the overwhelmingly Mormon and sometimes oppressive and conformist atmosphere of my school and town. I got in a lot of fights about religion and authority.

For some of my classmates, college was preordained. It was always understood that they would go to college, and that their families would help them pay for it. My circumstances were different. College was never mentioned as a real possibility for me, and there was definitely no money to pay for it. So I never thought of it as an option, and, aside from a couple of teachers, no one encouraged me in that direction.

This is not meant to be an excuse, but an explanation. I was angry, distracted, and self-destructive. But I am responsible for what I did. And I believe my rebelliousness was necessary in order for me to get through the circumstances of my life. While I take responsibility, I also make no apologies. I've moved on. And in some strange ways, the experience made me better, not less, equipped for college.

During all of this trouble, I maintained my desire for challenge and continued to take the most advanced courses offered at Middleton High School. Even if I didn't always perform at the top of my class, I always felt that it was with those minds where I belonged, and felt the most comfortable.

I could stand my ground in calculus and physics with any straight-A student, and I was very proud of that, because in many ways I was self-educated. Even if I didn't always come out looking the best, I always tried not to take the easy path. And sometimes I more than held my own—as in the state's Academic Decathlon, in English and other subjects where my curiosity and interest overcame my rebelliousness.

Since high school, I have maintained a voracious appetite for learning, from Dickens to Langston Hughes to writings about nanotechnology, chemistry, and biology. I have remained heavily involved in computing science, investigating and maintaining complex networks and studying everything from memes to artificial intelligence. I am not afraid of point of view, and am a sucker for almost any debate having to do with science, computing, or many aspects of politics and philosophy.

Out of this has come a rich and curious, if unsupervised and unstructured, education. An education taught by life, challenge, difficulty and will, born of my own spirit, and the spirit of the world in which I live and that I treasure. Never in the world would I replace the pleasure of reading a great author, or conquering some vast technical puzzle, for a perfect GPA.

But at the same time, I now want a different kind of education, a more structured one, and know how much I need it. I have lived entirely on my own in the world—something few nineteen-year-olds get to do—worked in an office tower, moved halfway across the country with no money or support in search of something.

A real education is what I've been looking for. I need it, and one way or another, I'll get it. I want it to be at the University of Chicago. I've read the school's catalogues, visited the campus, talked to students. I know it's the right place for me, the next step. I won't be disappointed if I come there, and I won't disappoint.

I don't have the words to explain to you how hard it is for me to sit and write this, to portray myself as if I were something special, as if I were not humble. Speaking about myself in such a tone is something that I find very hard to do. I don't believe in bragging, nor do I think that I am a genius of my own making.

What I do believe is that I can do this. I believe that I am smart enough, and know how to work hard enough, to make anything happen.

I'd like to enter the University of Chicago this fall. I'll need some help, financial and otherwise, but I can do it.

And I promise to do well by it, if I get the opportunity.

Sincerely,
Jesse Dailey

July 1997

Hey Katz,

As a project manager, I hold a lot of meetings that the geeks attend. It can be difficult to handle when you get a roomful of people, each with his or her own quirks. I have one who will show up 15 minutes late to every meeting, refuse to speak to anyone until we are getting up to leave, then start asking questions. Another one is ultra-insecure, she thinks everyone is trying to kick her off the team. Another is an absolute genius at software engineering but she is so overbearing to talk to that one client almost cancelled our entire contract. These people need a shield of nerds between them and the rest of society.

—Mark

THE DEAN

From: Jesse Dailey
To: Jon Katz

Hows it there? The weather is making me feel a little bit better, but I still feel like my life is beginning to plane off after a long, racing climb full of drastic change. And I don't feel good about it. I would hope that as I live my life, these brief periods will be just that, brief. That they will constitute a short impetus in which to rest and to gather courage and drive with which to move on, to inspire further change and growth. I don't know, maybe I need the distraction of constant movement. Maybe I won't ever be content with the present, and maybe I should be.

> > >

I WAS feeling particularly responsible for this situation: First I'd repeatedly urged Jesse to consider going to college, then I'd quailed at his decision to pursue one of the toughest.

At home, reality was seeping in. My daughter and her classmates were within weeks of getting their thin envelopes or fat ones. Some of her friends—students with solid academic records and all sorts of talents and accomplishments—had gotten shot down left and right as early applicants to schools like Brown, Amherst, and Yale. They and their families were in shock.

I was reading story after story about how difficult a year this was for college admissions, how selective the top schools had become, how even the brightest kids were meeting rejection.

Besides, the more I talked with Jesse, the more misgivings I had about how he would handle higher education. He was almost a wolf child, raised on his own for so long that he was ferociously independent, far more so than most twenty year olds.

Plus, there was a distinct twist to the evolution of a geek kid like Jesse: A significant part of his history, personality, education, and value system had been shaped by the Net where, by his own admission, he'd spent between twenty and forty hours a week for the past decade.

The Net had influenced him enormously, forming his libertarian mish-mash of political views, his suspicion of institutions and corporations, his eclectic interests in a thousand different subjects, his curious notions of intellectual and material property, and his penchant for developing ideas and theories in isolation.

Geeks who spend hours of their lives online, programming and gaming, practice what hackers call "deep magic": They enter a zone unique to the online world, where they are transfixed by the digital environment around them. Colleges, though most have invested in massive bandwidth to give their students easy access to the Net, remain collective enterprises. You study and live and socialize in a community.

From his series of computer perches, Jesse had grown up at odds with the conventional educational system. He had, like David Copperfield, been so long on his own that the ways of his peers were alien. Could he adjust to a communal learning process? Would he want to?

Taking full advantage of all the archived information that was never more than a few mouse clicks away, Jesse had strong ideas and theories about everything—the size of government, genetic engineering, gun control. Everyone who knew him, from Mr. Brown to his classmates, described him as fiercely opinionated. Would he be able to set his own ideas aside long enough to hear other people's?

What about that ingrained resentment toward yuppies, so strong he'd refused to even consider moving to some of the most interesting cities in America? Wouldn't he find himself surrounded by those kids whose parents had bought them their computers?

Jesse's gift—his equivalent of other kids' passion for music or sports—was computing. He didn't just talk about being a geek, it was his ideology, religion, identity. Was being "a geek on the rise" a valued asset at the University of Chicago, known for its classic core curriculum?

As I thought it through, I pictured a round of rejections—academic, social, cultural.

Money was an overriding factor. Jesse didn't have any to spare; neither did his parents. I had my own kid's tuition bills to face. Jesse would need nearly a full scholarship. Would he get it? Or be burdened with gigantic loans, years of obligations to finance an enterprise that would be difficult, at best?

One thing we had going for us was an excerpt from this book that ran in *Rolling Stone* in April 1999. Detailing Jesse and Eric's move from Idaho, it was headlined GEEKS: HOW TWO PISSED-OFF, CASTOFF NINETEEN-YEAR-OLDS ESCAPED A SEVEN-DOLLAR-AN-HOUR FUTURE IN DEAD-END IDAHO AND RODE THE INTERNET OUT OF TOWN. It traced Jesse and Eric's journey from Caldwell to Richton Park and ended with the Thanksgiving dinner we'd shared.

Predictably, the piece generated tons of e-mail and considerable interest online. Middle school girls put Jesse and Eric's picture up on their lockers; geeks, nerds, and hackers in Chicago e-mailed them. Just as predictably, the piece didn't really alter their social reality as I'd hoped. They were invited to a regular hacker get-together, went once, then never returned. They e-mailed some kids online and traded some MP3s; that was about the extent of it.

But the piece would at least give Jesse and Eric something to send to college admissions committees. It wouldn't make the difference between yea or nay, but it might attract some attention.

I'd called Kathy Anderson, the university's press officer, and sent her the magazine piece, asking if she could help put me in touch with the admissions people. She invited Jesse to the university for lunch. Afterward, impressed by his intelligence and curiosity, she said she'd do anything she could to help. The university had an interest in finding and nuturing promising "nontraditional" students, but it set very high standards as to who was sufficiently promising. She suggested I write the Dean of Admissions, Theodore O'Neill.

I'd taught at New York University for a few years, and had seen a bit of the academic bureaucracy. Perks were savagely guarded, even the tiniest territory defended to the death. The Chicago admissions office would not be looking for input from the press office or, for that matter, from a magazine writer.

I'd sent Dean O'Neill the article, with an accompanying letter. But I also understood that something more was required, a bold gesture. If anything, most academics would wrinkle their noses at a *Rolling Stone* piece.

Flying out to make a personal appeal might make him take notice. If I felt strongly enough about Jesse's deserving a shot— and I did—maybe such a trip would get his application a closer look or convince somebody in the admissions office that he was worth meeting.

It was an expensive undertaking on a dubious mission, but I would feel as if I'd done everything possible if I met with Dean O'Neill and made my pitch face to face.

In April, Jesse sent off the formal application that was due on January 1.

I called Dean O'Neill's office and made an appointment.

Each passing week made college—or some other break— feel more crucial. Jesse had shown all the heart, courage, and enterprise in the world, but he could see it wasn't getting him closer to where he wanted to be. He and Eric had the grit and skill that had propelled them out of Idaho, but grit and skill weren't working so well now. Jesse had made a couple of friends at work, and did go out sporadically; he was adventurous when he could be. But he needed to do something much more dramatic if he really wanted to break out.

He and Eric remained close, but they had been together day and night for nearly two years, gaming, networking, going to movies and out to dinner. Even for a young geek, that was a pretty small world. Jesse was more outgoing, increasingly restless, almost desperate for the books I'd occasionally send, or for word of a new movie.

He worried continually about Eric. Early on, his fear was that Eric was troubled and anxious about not finding work. "I think Eric is really feeling kinda bleak," he e-mailed me in November. "This is the same thing that happened last time he tried to be completely independent, when he went to Seattle. He ended up living off of and with his brother and never getting a job, and failing at interviews aplenty, and in general I think this has made him very afraid that the same thing will happen again . . . like maybe he thinks this is what is always going to happen."

This, Jesse noted, was a frightening position to be in. "Personally, I think there are just a few things he has not yet learned about life, and that is that you *cannot* get through it without learning how to communicate with people."

Now that Eric was working—and his job at Andersen was actually a little livelier than Jesse's, with more young people around—he was still feeling bleak, it seemed.

My relationship with Eric was warm, but he always seemed a little uneasy on the phone and his e-mail messages were occasional and spare. Whereas Jesse was energized by impossible challenges, Eric was discouraged by them. He was thinking a lot about programming, artificial intelligence (AI), and science. But his messages, in stark contrast to Jesse's feisty determination, were grim.

There was something hopeless in Eric's e-mail, like this response to my asking if he was liking work any better.

From: Eric P. Twilegar
To: Jon Katz

Yah, things are going a lot better, I'm just depressed. I think I'm going to go out to the blues fest tomorrow and have some blues to calm my nerves. I'm not sure though, I may just sit around and program while I have the time.

This whole brain thing is really having an effect on me. I'm not quite sure if it's good or bad. Everything from eating to seeing something gross is taking on a whole new meaning to me. I find myself analyzing every sensation, with every experience passing down the realization that I'm just a really fancy robot. . . . Everything has its downside, and in science it's starting to show. We may reveal the essence of our soul, but that's not necessarily a good thing. There needs to be some magic, there needs to be some conflict. This is going to be a major obstacle in AI I think. The robot will be totally aware of its own operations. It will know how to work because it will be able to read documentation describing it down to the last transistor. It takes the joys out of life, knowing everything has to suck.

Jesse hadn't lost his optimism yet. He almost always took a chance at socializing when he could. "I went out last night after work with a few coworkers to the bar in the lobby, it was kind of a going-away party for the telecommunications lady, who is leaving to go work for a start-up company for 20 percent more pay," he e-mailed me after one such foray. "It was fun, kind of the first chance I have had to get to know people around here a little.

There is one guy who might be considered a geek (he's into *South Park*, is an NT admin, loved *There's Something About Mary*), he's pretty cool outside of work, but on the job he's kind of a hard-ass, not too bad though."

He was always on the lookout for geeks and for the pop culture signifiers that were signs of geekhood (movies like *The Matrix* and *There's Something About Mary* being reliable indicators, almost passwords, along with TV shows like *The Simpsons* and, especially, *South Park*). But, he realized over time, he wasn't in an environment where he was likely to find many.

His constricted domestic routine, plus what he regarded as an often boring job, were becoming more suffocating as the novelty of being in Chicago wore off. Something had to give.

Around this time, he startled me by taking every penny he'd saved—about $1,300—and signing up for the 1999 Foresight Gathering, a weekend nanotechnology conference in San Jose, California, the capital of Silicon Valley.

Nanotechnology, a Jesse-obsession, was a subject matter so arcane and technical it's almost impossible for non-geeks to grasp. It's a hypothetical molecular-engineering technology in which objects are designed and built with the individual specification and placement of each separate atom. It's been a hot topic in the hacker subculture ever since the term was coined by K. Eric Drexler in his book *Engines of Creation,* in which he predicted that nanotechnology would permit an exponential growth of productivity and personal wealth.

Nanotechnologists literally seek to arrange atoms, and could, Drexler wrote, trigger the greatest technological breakthroughs of all time.

He posed the question in his book: "What would we build with those atom-stacking machines?" His answer: assemble machines much smaller than living cells, materials stronger and lighter than any available today. Thus, tiny devices that can travel along capillaries to enter and repair living tissue; the ability to heal disease, reverse the ravages of age, or make human bodies speedier and stronger than before. These new technologies could change the materials and means that shape the human environment.

To geeks, subjects like nanotechnology are like sports for other people. They can spend days and weeks debating the subject, trading information, arguing with one another on websites and mailing lists.

But here was a chance to chew it over with fellow geeks, face to face. The Foresight Gathering offered a heavy-duty lineup of digital and scientific thinkers: author and inventor Ray Kurzweil; open source pioneer and author of *The New Hacker's Dictionary* Eric S. Raymond; Drexler himself; and a variety of physicists, engineers, molecular biologists, and students. The conference had filled up months earlier, but Jesse managed to finagle his way in over the phone.

From: Jesse Dailey
To: Jon Katz

I'm back, and in excellent shape. . . . I had an absolute blast this weekend. . . . Completely awesome . . .

I'd wondered how Jesse would fit in with these cyber-heavyweights. It was astonishing that a kid who had yet to put

together his first date in Chicago would bankrupt himself—it
had taken him months to scrape that money together—to get to
a nanotechnology conference. But I'd never seen him so excited. Naturally, he loved spending the weekend arguing and
kicking around techno-ideas with people twice his age. I asked
for details.

From: Jesse Dailey
To: Jon Katz

Absolutely loved it . . . 150 people with three days of free
time to debate the future and everything between here and
there . . . had a very interesting talk with Eric Raymond
about open source, he's definitely got some very good reasons for why open development is going to take over the
world of software . . . a couple of good brain theories, lots
of social development debate . . .

It was awesome, I really wish I could capture some of the
magic in words . . . it was the magic of being in a room involved in active debate with 150 of the smartest people in the
world . . . the mathematicians and writers and physicists and
philosophers who you only get to read about, but being allowed to argue heatedly with them about all kinds of fas-
cinating things from "first-strike" scenarios to the moral
obligations of creating machine intelligence to living in a post-
scarcity economy . . .

From: Jon Katz
To: Jesse Dailey

This is why we need to get you into college . . .

The weekend, structured around a series of confidential panels, idea-sharing programs, and discussion groups, was vintage Jesse. He paid little attention to the surrounding Silicon Valley, though he'd never seen it before. He made no friends there, had no fun beyond talking and arguing, yet described the experience as the best time of his life. He had no hesitation about wading into battle over some aspect of nanotechnology with an esteemed physicist. It was a classic geek experience, in which the idea is everything, the environment irrelevant. "I loved the arguing, but I might have overdone it," he confessed later. "There was some silence at one point."

Inevitably, he was down when he returned to work the following Tuesday and was assigned to install some new hard drives. "It is so hard to be here after the weekend," he wrote me. "I think I might go out of my mind. Sitting here . . . well, it's a little discouraging." In Jesse-speak, "a little discouraging" meant profoundly depressing. My trip to Chicago to plead his case took on greater significance than ever.

If he got rejected at Chicago, would he muster the confidence to try again, perhaps at a slightly less selective school like Loyola or DePaul or the U of I? Or would he, as I suspected, deprive the yuppies of another crack at him and drift in some other direction?

On the flight, already unnerved by reading over a seatmate's shoulder about the awful school massacre in Littleton, Colorado, I felt increasingly uneasy, cataloguing all the very sound reasons for not having undertaken this trip. I was a presumptuous meddler. I was playing with natural outcomes, setting up an already battered kid for a big fall. The divide was too great now.

But Jesse was counting on me. Somebody had to speak for this kid and who better than me, the guy who'd been nosing around his life for the past six months?

The night before, I'd called and asked him if he really wanted to go through with this. He didn't hesitate. He knew all the risks but he wanted to apply. "I want to do something with my life besides fix computers in an office tower. I want to make a difference. I want to do interesting work, to be around ideas," he said. "I have to . . . otherwise . . ." He left the thought unfinished. The biggest fear in his mind, he said, was money. The university cost more than $30,000 a year; he couldn't imagine how he would get around that. Jesse dreaded debt and obligations.

As happened very occasionally in these late-night conversations, the cautious, guarded Jesse fell away. "Thank you for doing this," he said. "It means a lot to me. Working here has given me a window into the rest of my life. I know a lot about computers, but I don't know what to do with what I know. I don't have any real idea what I know or don't know. I don't have any context for it, you know, any idea where to go with it. I have to find out. Otherwise, I'll spend the rest of my life in Cubicleville.

"I want more. I really, really want more. I know now I have to go to college to do that. I didn't know it before. So I'd like you to come. If it's okay with you. If you want to." He added: "You can speak for me. You can explain me."

Making a direct plea was as painful as having his fingernails pulled out. I knew how hard it was for him to say what he'd just said. So early on the morning of April 21, I flew west and took a taxi to the University of Chicago for an 11 A.M. appointment with the Dean of Admissions.

IF THE University of Chicago was terra incognita for Jesse, it was also unsettling for me, not a world I was at ease in. Mediocre though it was, Jesse's high school transcript outshone mine. I remembered poor Mr. Hauser, who, in a meeting with my mother, broke down in tears of frustration at the prospect of teaching me ninth-grade algebra for the third—or was it fourth?—time. I'd spent my youth "not living up to my potential." I'd been bounced out of two different colleges, suspended for failing to attend class, for not completing the work.

Over the course of my adulthood, I'd had spectacular authority problems that dwarfed Jesse's. I'd worked for a dozen different employers, invariably storming out in a huff over one disagreement or another, before I'd gone into analysis, realized I didn't belong in institutions and needed to be my own boss, became a writer, worked at home to help take care of my kid, and more or less settled down. I had a visceral (and irrational) distrust of corporations and institutions like the University of Chicago. Though I wasn't a computing geek, I knew all about being an outsider looking in. It was, in fact, something Jesse and I shared completely.

We had the same view of people telling us what to write, think, or do. We didn't listen; we didn't do it. Why should any college take my word for Jesse's potential?

The day was gray and chilly. I had half an hour to kill, so I

wandered through the university bookstore, then got some coffee and sat outside on a stone bench, watching the parade of
undergraduates. I saw nose, cheek, eyebrow, and chin piercings. At least seven different shades of hair color that did not
occur in nature. The bulletin board was crammed with the an-
nouncements and activities of groups that didn't exist anywhere
near Caldwell, Idaho. And yes, there were definitely Jesse-like
computer geeks all over the place, heads hunched, laptops
bouncing on their shoulders, backpacks overstuffed.

It did not feel preppie, stuffy, or conformist. In fact, Jesse
would look straight here, almost like a Mormon, an irony I was
eager to torture him with. As much of an outsider as he is, Jesse
is personally surprisingly conservative. He rarely curses, drinks
moderately, and dresses as plainly as possible. Would he sprout
an earring if he came to a school like this? I couldn't picture it.
Still, settings like this had always been for other people, not me,
and I fought back some ancient fear and melancholia.

My cell phone warbled. Brian McLendon, a Random House
publicist who had become a friend, was wishing me luck—and
reporting more details of the Columbine High School shooting.
The response was already becoming hysterical—the shooters
were being described as computer geeks who played violent
games for many hours, were outcasts in their school, and had a
site on the Web. This of course described half the kids I knew.
When I checked my messages at home, Cate Corcoran, my former editor at the website Hotwired, had called to tell me that
some of my writings had been archived on the Trenchcoat
Mafia website, viewable until it was taken down by the authorities. When I got home, I knew I'd have a lot of e-mail.

I wondered how my media columns could possibly have found their way onto the website of the two kids who had just slaughtered so many of their classmates and themselves. I'd been writing online about geeks for several years. Perhaps that had something to do with it? Maybe I needed to write something about this.

But now, I had to focus on this meeting.

I had never had a college admissions interview and couldn't have been more nervous if this were my own. I smoothed my sparse hair, tucked my shirt in, flicked some dog hair off my navy jacket.

The admissions office was in a literally ivy-covered hall, a Gothic-looking building that practically screamed Major University! It also yelled: You haven't got a chance, bud.

Before I went in, feeling jangled from the coffee I'd been chugging since dawn, I called Jesse and arranged to have lunch with him afterward.

"Wish me luck," I said.

"Luck," Jesse said, never one for excessive verbalizing about feelings. But then, there wasn't a need to say much.

The receptionist seemed puzzled about exactly who I was and what I was doing there, but was mollified by the fact that I did have an appointment. I sat on a plush sofa with an excellent view of the conference area where applicants and their parents come to meet with counselors. A series of parents with nervous kids in tow sat at oak tables and asked questions about the school. The parents seemed to do all of the talking; the kids were glazed-looking, nearly mute.

Everyone was dauntingly well dressed. I overheard references to daunting GPAs, too, and to horseback riding championships and symphony orchestras. These were, in fact, the very yuppies Jesse had gone to such lengths to avoid.

What were the odds that the people running this school would actually bestir themselves to make room for Jesse? The deck felt thoroughly stacked. We would see how nontraditional they were prepared to be.

A tall man who appeared to be in his early forties, with a shock of silvery hair, wheeled an aluminum bike into a paneled office, then reemerged to greet me. Dean O'Neill looked every bit the classic academic in khakis and a blue shirt. He seemed pleasant but wary, almost bewildered. When I introduced myself and asked him if he'd read the *Rolling Stone* article I'd sent on Jesse and Eric's trek from Idaho, he said he hadn't. This wasn't a good beginning.

In fact, as politely as he could, O'Neill asked me who the hell I was. I explained that I was an author and media writer doing a book on geeks—his eyes widened at the term—and that I had been writing for several years about the Net and the Web. He told me that, other than e-mail, he had never really spent any time on the Net. This also wasn't a great sign.

We circled for a moment, each of us trying to gauge how much trouble the other might make. He didn't seem to want to talk that much about Jesse. But I perked up when he said he was teaching a class on the Enlightenment. I'd just written a series of articles for Slashdot, comparing the Enlightenment and the Internet. Many of the most stirring ideas of Enlightenment philosophers—freedom of information, intellectual autonomy, a broad inclusiveness about ideas, a willingness to reach beyond conventional wisdom and dogma—were being played out on the Net, I told him. It turned out we were both drawn to the same Enlightenment thinker, David Hume. O'Neill said he wanted to understand the Net better, and was aware how much the students and faculty were talking about it and using it.

He had been feeling me out, I realized, trying to grasp exactly what I was doing there. We were, I sensed, going to cut to the chase.

I told him about the book I was working on. I handed him a copy of the magazine article, with its photo of a serious-looking Jesse and Eric, and explained that the clean shaven one was, as of a few days ago, an applicant. I apologized for the lateness of the application, and warned that Jesse's grades weren't great, probably well below the standard University of Chicago hopeful's.

He seemed taken aback when I explained that I'd come from New Jersey to make a case for Jesse and told me what I already knew: The university had had a record jump in applications this year.

"Look," I said, leaning forward. "I made this trip because it was the most convincing argument I can make for how strongly I feel about Jesse, about my belief that he belongs here, that he is smart enough to do the work, and has enough character. If you take a chance on him, you will get paid back in spades. And he will pay the world back by contributing something special to it."

O'Neill listened carefully while I went through Jesse's story: his family's involvement in a religious cult when he was young, the three divorces he'd lived through, his father's illness. While kids like my daughter were piling up grades and accomplishments, Jesse was joining a gang, dabbling in drugs, battling Mormons, school administrators, and conformity.

He also, I said, lived in a digital world. I explained how I'd seen Jesse install operating systems, play online games from chess to Quake, use astonishing ingenuity to gather archived information off the Web.

"I want you to know if you admit Jesse, I will stick with him," I said. "I will be here for the duration. He'll need support, and I'll provide it. I won't walk away from him."

I read a bit from two of Jesse's essays. I even explained the origins of the term "geek," how so many of them, once destined to be marginalized outcasts, were using technology to alter their fates, change their destinies, build a new culture.

O'Neill interrupted with questions from time to time. He asked more about my notions of the Net as a second Enlightenment. He wondered about the impact of the Net on traditional cultural enclaves, like academe. He conceded that it was important, but he was skeptical.

He didn't say much about Jesse, except that he would be willing to meet with him. It sounded like Jesse didn't have much of a paper trail to bring to the admissions committee, however. And, he added ominously, it was very late. Was Jesse actually applying for the fall?

I tried to explain the circumstances, the sudden move from Idaho. "Jesse has been in an office tower since October," I added, as I prepared to leave. "He's seen something of the world. He understands what a college education means, what the alternatives are. Somebody needs to take a chance on this kid. If he doesn't make the move now, he might head off in a different direction."

O'Neill nodded noncommittally and walked me out of the building and two blocks to the nearest cab stand. If I were in Chicago again, I should drop by; he'd love to have me sit in on his Enlightenment class. Our conversation had been interesting, helpful.

Like Jesse after he's been forced to talk too long, I was spent. O'Neill had been gracious and attentive, but there was no reason to believe Jesse was an inch closer to getting into school.

In Lakeview, Jesse was waiting for me—though he was, of course, online. I understood his particular style of greeting, by now: He'd buzz me into the Cave, leaving the door ajar. When I walked in, he'd be sitting at his computer with his back to me. He'd yell hi, then clack away for a few minutes, while I took out my notebook and strolled through the place, playing writer and cataloguing the apartment's meager contents. I'd ask if he was hungry. Sure, he'd say, and he'd log off whatever program he was on, throw on a jacket, leave the computer running, and walk out with me.

This time the apartment was exactly as I'd last seen it, except the Katz Diet Coke can was gone, consumed by the forlorn friend from Idaho.

We went to a Japanese restaurant, and I filled Jesse in on the not-so-positive news.

The dean, I said, had been polite, but he didn't seem to quite know who Jesse was. "I guess the fact that he didn't throw me out of his office is a good sign," I said lamely. "I mean, if there were no chance whatsoever, he would have probably told me." I told Jesse that O'Neill would be expecting his call, that the next move was his. But frankly, I said, I wouldn't get my hopes up.

Three weeks later, Jesse met with Dean O'Neill. I called that night to see how it went.

"Reasonably well," he said. "Ted's a cool guy." Ted?

They'd gotten into an extended argument about free will, Jesse said, which was cool. Jesus, I thought, Jesse took on a University of Chicago dean over free will? What kind of argument?

"Well, he was completely wrong," Jesse said. "We argued about whether or not there exists a faculty of reason unique to man. Whether man is the only beast capable of true reasoning. I argued that no, there is no such thing as reason, just chemistry and electricity . . . the mind is just a mass of chemicals and electricity. There's nothing magic about it. There's absolutely no spiritual consciousness that allows us to be more deeply reasoning than other creatures in the world."

O'Neill, Jesse said, was teaching his Enlightenment course that day, so the subject had been on his mind. He disagreed, as Jesse recounted it, but then conceded that he really "couldn't argue with my science."

Was that what they talked about? Mostly, said Jesse. He'd talked about his life and school record, and the Dean had asked if he'd finished high school at all. He seemed relieved that he had. Otherwise, they'd spent most of an hour in their free will battle, which Jesse said was "awesome."

The geeks versus the Enlightenment. I bet O'Neill had poured himself a stiff drink at lunch afterward.

What did he say at the end? I asked.

"He said he didn't know whether I could be admitted or not, but that he'd love to have me in his humanities class."

GEEK VOICES

July 1997

Hello Jon,

You could say the majority of Americans were always geeks, until we got post-Depression urbanization and illusions of sophistication. We looked like Dorothy's Kansas friends in *The Wizard Of Oz* and we admired Tom Edison and his good old gumption and stick-to-itiveness. What a geek. You've got to have obscure but essential technology before geekdom can be cool, however. You don't really start admiring geek qualities until one of them saves your ass by bringing back your corporate LAN or fixing the missile telemetry. Maybe NASA really started the elevation of geek culture.

—Jeff

From: Jesse Dailey
To: Jon Katz

Exactly prior to the Geek Club era, I went through my rebellious phase and got pretty heavy into drugs and got involved in a gang. . . . It was that whole seeking-out thing that eventually landed me in the Geek Club. . . .

A guy in Nampa (who was a loose friend of ours) walked into the front door of our mutual enemies and shot him and his brother point blank in the face, killed A and vegetabled his brother; 3 of us put 4 bullet holes in the back of a van that was speeding away from us. Things during that time were pretty fucked up, I was big into amphetamines and acid, and I couldn't think very straight at all. . . .

I would say that that was one of the most important changes that technology made, was that it helped me to wake up out of that, during all this I was still big into computers at home, and I was always the guy who fucked with all the stolen computer shit, and when I started being involved in the Geek Club, I kinda started seeing how shitty of an existence that would have been.

Photo taken in Kalamazoo, Michigan,
shortly after the Columbine shootings.
SIMON KING

> > >

FOR THE alienated, brainy, oddball young souls of the world, there was life before the Internet and life after. Had he been born twenty years earlier, Jesse would have probably suffered the traditional geeks' fate in school, then slunk home to read comics and watch some bad TV. If he were lucky, Eric would have watched with him.

But life for geeks has been transformed. For one thing, they aren't alone anymore. They probably still loathe school, but when they go home, their computers are passports to a vast, complex, and communicative world, one still largely invisible to many parents, educators, and other adults.

High priests in journalism and culture are fond of fussing that the Internet is dislocating, isolating, dangerous. After spending so much time online, talking to so many kids like Jesse and Eric, I view it differently. It isn't the Net that drives kids into isolation or creates lonely children; the Net attracts lonely and ignored kids, and puts them in touch with others just like them.

Jesse has spent more time in this world than in any other for much of his life—since the fifth grade, he guesses. It has shaped him as much or more than any other cultural, social, or educational force, or combination thereof.

When the *Idaho Statesman* ran its feature on Internet-obsessed kids in 1995, with Jesse as the Net-addict poster boy, he told the reporter he spent thirty-five to forty hours a week on the Net. "His favorite spot is the inter-relay chat site, where he talks with friends for five to six hours a night during the week, usually until 3 A.M. on Saturday and noon to 10 P.M. on

Sunday," the paper noted. If anything, Jesse spends more time online now; the things that draw him there—games, weblogs, chat and messaging systems, open source operating programs—have become far more advanced and compelling.

Such kids don't suffer alone anymore. They tell their stories to one another almost continuously, via twenty-four-hour, seven-day-a-week messaging systems much more advanced than the IRC in the *Statesman*'s story. Programs like ICQ and Hotline make it simple to set up communities of like-minded people with shared interests. These programs open windows on a computer screen that stay open day and night.

For geeks, these are the real news media. Jesse spends much of his time on Hotline, talking to friends all over the country and around the world about music, software, sometimes actual news. Such friends are invisible, but they exist.

The rest of the time, these kids go to school, do homework, and sleep in their beds every night. But in their hearts and souls, they dwell in the geek nation. And ignorance of that alternative world is dangerous, sometimes putting both its citizens and society at peril.

At lunch on the day of my Chicago visit, Jesse and I could hardly stop talking about what had happened at Littleton. There was much more to say about it than about my inconclusive session with Dean O'Neill. Somehow, Jesse had escaped that degree of anger and disconnection. But he'd brushed against it, come close. There but for the grace of God . . .

He'd never kill anybody, Jesse said firmly. But he had to admit he felt some sympathy for the two young killers, if none for their brutal actions. He'd walked a way in those shoes, he said.

Now he could see what was coming. "You wait, they'll blame the geeks," he predicted, meaning the general "they" of the media and its alleged experts. "They'll blame computer games and the Net. Life for geeks like me who are still in high school will be hell. . . . It probably already is."

I ran for my plane, telling Jesse I'd call him that night. After our discussion, I thought I should write something about this, maybe for Slashdot, the techno-centered website that was among geeks' favorite gathering spots. I was also thinking that, as cooler observers around me had been cautioning, it would probably be saner, cheaper, and easier for Jesse to try for the University of Illinois in the fall. He was preparing for that shift in strategy. At lunch, we'd agreed to go on the U of I's website that week to look at the courses and application process.

By that evening, when I called Jesse, the news from and about Columbine was already confirming his predictions. "Computer games: how they may be turning your kids into killers!" was the promo on one New York newscast. The cable channels were filling with moral guardians, politicians, pundits, and therapists warning about computer games like Doom (which the Columbine killers played) and about hate material on the Net (the killings took place on Adolf Hitler's birthday). We heard warnings about black clothes and white makeup, Goth music, computer addictions. We learned various warning signals of youthful disconnection and disturbances. "They" were describing geeks.

Net hysteria, a staple of modern journalistic and political life, flares up whenever there's a killing, sex assault, new virus, hacking incident, or other problem even remotely connected to the Internet.

These hysterias are well known to anybody who spends any time online, though the incidents are extraordinarily rare when viewed in proportion to total Net and Web use. But every geek has had a brush with a parent, a teacher, a clergyman, someone who's branded his or her Net passion dangerous, unhealthy, addictive, or bizarre. When Jesse and a few friends started playing computer games in the Middleton High library at lunchtime, nervous parents forced the librarian to make them stop.

None of this was awfully far in his past and, as we talked about Columbine, the anger bubbled up, still fresh. He'd spent a few hours on media and geek sites that evening, gauging the reaction to the Littleton kids who'd been dubbed the Trenchcoat Mafia.

The horror stories were already pouring in, Jesse reported: kids sent home for wearing trench coats or black clothing, ordered into counseling for playing games like Quake and Doom.

"If I were in high school," Jesse sputtered, "I would show up in a trench coat and fedora. I'd wear them every single day. I would make them suspend me, by God. I would fight them every step of the way, the arrogant sons of bitches."

After a while, he calmed down. "You never want to hurt anybody," he explained. "But there were a lot of days when I was at Middleton that I'm glad I didn't have a gun around. It's a piecemeal, gradual, daily grinding down of you as a human. First, there's the school, where you have to leave the Constitution and all your rights at the door. They tell you what to think, where to sit, what to wear. They tell you what you can and can't read. They try to tell you what to think.

"The whole school is set up for other people—jocks and preppies, sports. You are not valued at all. You are constantly

taunted, humiliated, elbowed, laughed at. The classes are boring and most of the teachers don't care if you live or die. People hate you for having ideas, for talking about them, for being
different. You are never—ever—invited to anything. High
school is like a whole universe of parties, groups, activities to
which you are the only person who doesn't have the key, who
never gets an invitation.

"You start to get angry, then you start to hate. They just slice
away your humanity, piece by piece, and the hate becomes bigger and bigger, until there's nothing left but hate. If you don't
have good friends or a teacher or a parent to talk to, then one
day, there's just no humanity left. You're *all* hate. You have no
connection to the world. And so you snap." This anger is always
near the surface in Jesse, even now.

What had rescued Jesse was the camaraderie of the Geek
Club, one sympathetic teacher, a sense of mastery from his computing skills, and the ability to talk with his sister and mother.

But the parallels to Eric Harris and Dylan Klebold, the sui-
cidal gunmen, were frightening and eerie. *The New York Times*
subsequently reported that the two had performed well in
class, but remained far on the outskirts of the social scene. And
there was this: "Expert computer programmers who configured
games like Doom to their own specifications, the two were
once suspended for hacking into the school mainframe. But the
boys also helped maintain Columbine's Linux server, and
taught classmates how to download from the Internet." That
could as easily have been written about Jesse or Eric.

By now, extensive talks with them and with hundreds of
geeks online had given me some insight into the alienation

rampant in geek culture. So I wrote the first in a series of Slash-dot columns we called the "Hellmouth" series.

Slashdot is a center for the open source and free software movements. Nearly ten years ago, Linus Torvalds, then a student in Finland, developed a computer operating system called Linux, which was collectively improved by geeks all over the world and distributed free to anyone who wanted it. The only restrictions were that improvements had to be shared at no cost. The open source movement has grown to more than eight million users, perhaps the geekiest social movement on the Net, since its members and passionate adherents are program-mers and designers. They would understand something about alienated youth.

"The Hellmouth," the entry point for evil in the world, is a term recently popularized by the geek-beloved TV series *Buffy the Vampire Slayer*; its witty central conceit is high school as Hellmouth, entryway into this world for vampires, ghouls, and predators.

The following is an abridged version of the first column to run after the Columbine massacre. It brought an avalanche of e-mail, the first of which came from Jesse: "Brav-fucking-O. you really hit the nail on the head with this one!"

FROM THE HELLMOUTH

THE BIG story never seemed to quite make it to the front pages or the TV talk shows. It wasn't whether the Net is a place for hate-mongers and bomb-makers, or whether video games are turning your kids into killers. It was the spotlight the Littleton, Colorado, killings has put on the fact that for so many individualistic, intelligent, and vulnerable kids, high school is a Hellmouth of exclusion, cruelty, loneliness, inverted values, and rage.

From *Buffy the Vampire Slayer* to Todd Solondz's *Welcome to the Dollhouse,* and a string of comically bitter teen movies from Hollywood, pop culture has been trying to get this message out for years. For many kids—often the best and brightest—school is a nightmare.

People who are different are reviled as geeks, nerds, dorks. The lucky ones are excluded, the unfortunates are harassed, humiliated, sometimes assaulted literally as well as socially. Odd values—unthinking school spirit, proms, jockhood—are exalted, while the best values—free thinking, nonconformity, curiosity—are ridiculed. Maybe the one positive legacy the Trenchcoat Mafia left was to ensure that this message got heard by a society that seems desperate not to hear it.

I've gotten a steady stream of e-mail from middle- and high-school kids all over the country, kids in trouble or who see themselves that way to one degree or another in the hysteria sweeping the country after the shootings in Colorado.

Many of these kids felt like targets of a new hunt for oddballs—suspects in a bizarre, systematic search for the strange and the alienated. Suddenly, in this tyranny of the normal, to be different wasn't just to feel unhappy, it was to be dangerous.

Schools all over the country openly embraced "Geek Profiling." One group calling itself the National School Safety Center issued a checklist of "dangerous signs" to watch for in kids. It included mood swings, a fondness for violent TV or video games, cursing, depression, antisocial behavior and attitudes. (I don't know about you, but I bat a thousand.)

The panic was fueled by a ceaseless bombardment of powerful, televised images of mourning and grief in Colorado, images that stir the emotions and demand some sort of response, even when it isn't clear what the problem is.

The reliably blockheaded media response didn't help. *Sixty Minutes* devoted a whole hour to screen violence and games' supposedly lethal impact on the young. The already embattled loners were besieged.

"This is not a rational world. Can anybody help?" asked Jamie, head of an intense Dungeons and Dragons club in Minnesota, whose school guidance counselor gave him a choice: give up the game or face counseling, possibly suspension. Suzanne Angelica (her online handle) was told to go home and leave her black, ankle-length raincoat there.

On *Star Wars* and *X-Files* mailing lists and websites and on AOL chat rooms and ICQ message boards, teenagers traded countless stories of being harassed, ostracized, and ridiculed by teachers, students, and administrators for dressing and thinking differently from the mainstream. A few even wrote of being beaten. Many said they had some understanding of why the killers in Littleton went over the edge.

"We want to be different," one of the Colorado killers declared in a diary found by the police. "We want to be strange and we don't want jocks or other people putting us down." The sentiment, if not the response to it, was echoed by kids all over the country. Now the Littleton killings have made their lives much worse.

"I'm a Quake freak, I play it day and night. I'm really into it. I play Doom a lot too, though not so much anymore. I'm up till 3 A.M. every night. I really love it," e-mailed Brandy from New York City. "But after Colorado, things got horrible. People were actually talking to me like I could come in and kill them. It wasn't like they were really afraid of me—they just seemed to think it was okay to hate me even more. . . . People asked me if I had guns at home. This is a whole new level of exclusion, another excuse for the preppies of the universe to put down and isolate people like me."

The e-mailed stories ranged from suspensions and expulsions for "antisocial behavior" to censorship of student publications to new restrictions on computing, Web browsing, and especially gaming. Everywhere, school administrators pandered and panicked, rushing to show they were highly sensitive to parents' fears, even if they were oblivious to the needs and problems of many of their students.

Few of the week's media reports—in fact, none that I saw—pointed out what the FBI Uniform Crime Reports, issued biannually, along with Justice Departments reports, academic studies, and some news stories have reported for years now: Violence among the young is dropping across the country, even as computing, gaming, cable TV, and other media use rises.

Unhappy, alienated, isolated kids are legion in schools, and voiceless in media, education, and politics. But theirs are the most important voices of all in understanding what happened and perhaps even how to keep it from happening again.

I referred some of my e-mailers to peacefire.org, a children's rights website, for help in dealing with blocking and filtering software. I sent others to the website Free! (freedomforum.org) for help with censorship and free speech issues, and to geek websites, especially on ICQ.com where kids can talk freely.

I've also chosen some e-mail to partially reprint here. Although almost all of these correspondents were willing to be publicly identified—some demanded it—I'm using only their online names, since their stories could put them in peril from parents, peers, or school administrators.

From Jay in the Southeast:

I stood up in a social studies class—the teacher wanted a discussion—and said I could never kill anyone or condone anyone who did kill anyone. But that I could, on some level, understand these kids in Colorado, the killers. Because day after day, slight after slight, exclusion after exclusion, you can learn how to hate, and that hatred grows and takes you over sometimes, especially when you come to see that you're hated only because you're smart and different, or sometimes even because you are online a lot, which is still so uncool to many kids. . . .

After the class, I was called to the principal's office and told that I had to agree to undergo five sessions of counseling or be expelled from school, as I had expressed "sympathy" with the killers in Colorado, and the school had to be able to explain itself if I "acted out." In other words, for speaking freely, and to cover their ass, I was not only branded a weird geek, but a potential killer. That will sure help deal with violence in America.

From Anika78 in suburban Chicago:

I was stopped at the door of my high school because I was wearing a trench coat. I don't game, but I'm a geekchick, and I'm on the Web a lot. (I love geek guys, and there aren't many of us.) I was given a choice—go home and ditch the coat, or go to the principal. I refused to go home. I have never been a member of any group or trench coat mob or any hate thing, online or any other, so why should they tell me what coat to wear?

Two security guards took me into an office, called the school nurse, who was a female, and they ordered me to take my coat off. The nurse asked me to undress (privately) while the guards outside the door went through every inch of my coat. I wouldn't undress, and she didn't make me (I think she felt creepy about the whole thing).

Then I was called into the principal's office and he asked me if I was a member of any hate group, or any online group, or if I had ever played Doom or Quake. He mentioned some other games, but I don't remember them. I'm not a gamer, though my boyfriends have been. I lost it then. I thought I was going to be brave and defiant, but I just fell apart. I cried and cried. I think I hated that worse than anything.

From ES in New Jersey:

High school favors people with a certain look and attitude—the adolescent equivalent of Aryans. They are the chosen ones, and they want to get rid of anyone who doesn't look and think the way they do. One of the things which makes this so infuriating is that the system favors shallow people. Anyone who took the time to think about things would real-ize that things like the prom, school spirit, and who won the football game are utterly insignificant in the larger scheme of things.

So anyone with depth of thought is almost automatically excluded from the main high school social structure. It's like some horribly twisted form of Social Darwinism.

I would never, ever do anything at all like what was done in Colorado. I can't understand how anyone could. But I do understand the hatred of high school life which, I guess, prompted it.

From Jip in New England:

Dear Mr. Katz. I am 10. My parents took my computer away today, because of what they saw on television. They told me they just couldn't be around enough to make sure that I'm doing the right things on the Internet. My mom and dad told me they didn't want to be standing at my funeral someday because of things I was doing that they didn't know about. I am at my best friend's house, and am pretty bummed, because things are boring now. I hope I'll get it back.

I was stunned by the flood of e-mail and media attention this column and those that followed soon generated. Unhappy kids now have a medium in which they can express, instantaneously and eloquently, the reality of their lives, both to one another and to the rest of the world. They used it.

Slashdot, which typically gets hundreds of thousands of hits a day, crashed repeatedly under the weight of all the people, mostly high school kids, trying to post messages about the column, not only that day but every day I passed along stories from the Hellmouth. For all of the messages that were posted or sent, thousands more never got through.

Soon, I was besieged by reporters from TV networks, radio news organizations, and newspapers, all wanting to write about what I called "geek profiling," trying to get in touch with the kids who were e-mailing me, anxious to talk to kids who'd been punished, sent home for dressing oddly, suspended or otherwise singled out for daring to be different or—worst of all—for daring to express any sympathy or understanding for two killers. Several journalists, at my suggestion, posted messages on Slashdot, asking kids to contact them.

The columns were entered into the Congressional Record, linked to and reprinted on websites and mailing lists all over the world. They got distributed in high schools, posted on college bulletin boards. Daily newspapers reprinted parts of them as op-ed columns or quoted from them in editorials. They made their way to worried parents, usually at the hands of their children, who printed out and turned over the writings they hoped would help explain.

The message was getting out, and teachers and administrators were hearing it. The geek kids had done something remarkable, it seemed to me, and quite unprecedented: They had used their medium, the Net, to join the national debate and had altered the direction of a major story—one that was, thanks to knee-jerk journalists and opportunistic politicians, threatening to become a witch-hunt.

For me, the messages were raw and painful. I couldn't stop reading them, alternating between rage and sorrow; it was like having my skin rubbed off. Every time I turned my e-mail program on, I faced hundreds of messages from kids, students, former students, parents, and teachers stacked in vast queues; it took hours just to download the mail. My computer wobbled under the strain; I had to replace it, losing several e-mail programs in the process. A couple of days later I fled to upstate New York, where I own a small cabin that serves as a writing retreat. I brought my laptop, which soon also labored under the e-mail onslaught.

These kids seemed so smart and articulate, almost passionately idealistic, and they seemed to be suffering so pointlessly. Now, along with feeling lonely and humiliated, they had all become suspects.

Determined to answer their e-mail, I took to eating meals at my computer (not good for keyboards) and hardly left the house.

Some of the voices were so plaintive and compelling I couldn't get them out of my head. I referred several of the most unnerving cases to the teachers, social workers, and other older geeks who'd volunteered to help. Within a few days, we had an informal online counseling service under way, trying to send kids who seemed to be in serious trouble to sympathetic parents or professionals.

The experience was extraordinary. As *The New York Times* pointed out, Slashdot had become the focal point for geek misery in America, a subcultural phenomenom that crystallized post-Littleton and, thanks to the Net and Web, had become part of the dialogue.

It seems taken for granted in America that life for idiosyncratic, individualistic kids is brutal. Several critics wrote dismissively that these were just spoiled middle-class children whining about their privileged places in life. I can say with utter conviction that nothing could have been further from the truth. An electronic river of true pain had sprung up in that period of national soul-searching, far deeper than I'd imagined, and it was wrenching to have so much of it run literally through my fingers.

From police in a Massachusetts town, I heard of a fourteen-year-old boy sitting in his bedroom with his father's shotgun in his mouth, a computer screen open to Slashdot. His life was simply unbearable, for all the usual reasons, and the Columbine coverage persuaded him it would only get worse. It took the cops and other frightened adults three hours to persuade him to put the gun down. It was an incident I declined to share with Slashdot readers, nor did I tell them about a fifteen year old in the Midwest with a history of emotional problems who e-mailed me every day for weeks after Columbine asking for help. He routinely had his books stolen, got punched and kicked, was laughed at when he spoke in class and ignored by teachers; for him, there was no Mr. Brown. He said he had twice tried suicide.

In the charged atmosphere after Littleton, it struck me as unwise to circulate such extreme stories among kids who already felt vulnerable and angry. Yet it was a reminder of what relentless harassment and exclusion could, in some cases, produce.

I forwarded many of these e-mails to Jesse, which was wrenching for both of us. We talked nearly continuously, via phone and e-mail, about what to tell individual kids. I passed along his exhortations to endure, and to use the Net to make friendly connections. "Tell them to hang on," Jesse advised. "High school can be hell, but there is life beyond, and tell them that on the Net, we geeks are not alone anymore."

He knew what they were feeling. He recounted time after time how he would break every rule at Middleton High, speak openly about the persecution that sometimes led to violence, wear clothes calculated to upset the school administration, make statements that drove the Mormon majority crazy. He'd been a provocateur.

Yet he was among several friends and advisers cautioning me that perhaps I had written enough. Rob Malda, the founder of Slashdot, was also urging me to stop. The site was crashing under the traffic, and Slashdot had had to cut off public posts after the first two hundred to keep from being overwhelmed. In fact, Rob was deliberately running other stories and links ahead of my columns, in order to get some information out before the site went down as readers rushed to respond. My family was growing concerned about my haunted look; I was having trouble sleeping.

But like it or not, I was the conduit, the transmitter. There seemed no end to these stories, or to their power. The second column, also abridged:

VOICES FROM THE HELLMOUTH

THE MESSAGES started coming in a trickle Friday afternoon, then a torrent by Monday. They were wrenching, sometimes astonishing, an electronic outpouring of breathtaking anger and compassion.

These painful testimonials explained more—a lot more— about Littleton than all the vapid media stories about video violence, Goths, game-crazed geeks.

For a writer, there's nothing more humbling than to be at a loss for words. I can't possibly do more justice to some of these posts than to let them speak for themselves.

By last night, I had received thousands of e-mails about

school. Few remembered it fondly—none, in fact. Some had unbearable memories. Some are still recovering. Many more are still there, suffering every day.

Many of you wrote asking if you could help these kids. Others wondered if there was any way to get the message about their lives out beyond Slashdot, if these stories might reach the mainstream media in some form.

Don't worry about that. The column and the responses to it ricocheted all over the world, via e-mail, mailing lists, links, even faxes. There were scores of requests to reprint. For any others, and on behalf of Slashdot, be my guest.

On the Net, ideas don't need to be pushed. They find their own audience and stand or fall of their own weight. Eventually, I will answer each e-mail, and am grateful for them.

Here are more voices from the Hellmouth, from some of its children:

From rpacker:

Hellmouth has become the Stonewall for us geeks.

It marks the point where we stopped running and hiding and waiting, and stopped and stood our ground. From this point on we make our voices heard.

From Jennifer in Alabama:

Katz, I just finished reading "More Stories from the Hellmouth," and it left me speechless. I never knew that so many people experienced the same misery I am going through right now, and I want to thank you for giving them a chance to speak out.

I am currently a senior in high school. In fifteen days I will graduate and leave these prison-gray walls, but I'll always carry the memories with me.

I'm a Goth/Wiccan in Alabama, and for the crime of wearing black lipstick, a trench coat, and a pentagram, I've been a social outcast for four years. In some ways I've had it better than many of your respondents: I'm graduating at the top of my class as a National Merit Scholar with a 1600 SAT, a finalist for the Alabama All-State Academic Team and a semifinalist for the Presidential Scholars, among other things. I spent last summer studying at Harvard University, and in September I'll matriculate at Yale University. I hold these things up as talismans to protect me; all my awards are thin paper shields to keep me safe from the hatred that surrounds me and my friends.

Because I attend a large public high school in a state where football is idolized and jocks are demigods, I've had my fair share of abuse. But because I'm a girl and the academic star of my class, many kindhearted teachers have gone out of their way to protect me. I have never been physically shoved around or beaten, but I have had to endure frothy-mouthed harangues from Bible-thumping fanatics, and I have been cursed at, shunned, and mocked openly.

It hurts. I'm so glad that Littleton happened at the end of my senior year. I wouldn't be able to endure much more of this. Why do people feel justified in making negative assumptions instead of positive ones? Why do they assume that a kid in a black trench coat must be a psychotic murderer instead of a National Merit Scholar? Isn't the administration aware that if they continue these repressive policies, all the best students will desert the school faster than rats from a sinking ship? *We* are the ones who earn their state grants; *we* are the ones who make this place a nationally recognized Blue Ribbon School— and *we* are the ones who are being alienated.

The hysteria has gotten so intense here that a Muslim girl was sent home for wearing a black veil over her hair.

And the thing that stings most, to me, is that I'm so helpless to stop the madness. I am a leader, of sorts, among the tiny Goth community in my school, and yet there does not seem to be any effective action I can take. What can I do? I want to speak out, but I have no venue to voice my protest. I'm planning a speech/demonstration at next week's senior celebration, but that seems such a small and impotent gesture. . . . What I want, more than anything, is a chance to go up and *tell* the school officials of America that they are shooting themselves in the foot here.

Please do that. You speak for us; take our stories and let them know what is happening here.

From John, age thirty-seven:

What this really means to all my fellow young geeks out there? Endure. It may take a year, or two or five, but we will win. . . . All those preps, jocks, etc., etc., will have their M.R.S. degrees, 2.5 kids, a job at Circuit City as an assistant manager, will be wondering where their life went, when we are coming into full bloom and taking over the world.

From Peter in Boston:

I am a geek, and very proud of it. I am beaten, spit on, pushed, jeered at. Food is thrown at me while teachers pretend not to see, people trip me. Jocks knock me down in the hallway. They steal my notes, call me a geek and a fag and a freak, tear up my books, have pissed in my locker twice. They cut my shirt and rip it. They wait for me in the boys' room and beat me up. I have to wait an hour to leave school to make sure they're gone.

Mostly, I honestly think, this is because I'm smarter than they are, and they hate that.

The really amazing thing is, they are the most popular people in the school, while everybody thinks I'm a freak for being online and playing computer games. The teachers just slobber all over them. Mostly, the other kids laugh, or walk away and pretend not to see it. The whole school cheers when they play sports. Sometimes, I want very much to kill them. Sometimes, I picture how I'd do it. Wouldn't you? But unlike those guys in Littleton, I never will. I value my own life much more. When I read these messages, I would ask other geeks to try and remember that, no matter what. And get online and make contact.

From Evan:

I am 24 years old, and a successful professional now, but ten years ago, I was in the Hellmouth. Just wanted to shout some small form of encouragement out to the kids fighting today.

Take your fight for the right to be different to the people with power, and enlist your parents' help. Remember that if you can get your parents to understand your need to be creative, and nonconformist, because your brain is just plain bigger than the small world of middle and high school, your parents can make a fuss to school boards. But if they won't listen, go to the school boards yourself. Peacefully, but forcefully, assert your right to be different by speaking out against fear and oppression. Because that's what it is. It's all about the fear.

People fear what they don't understand, and let's face it, the world of a geek isn't something most people can understand, if only because it's a complicated world filled with smart folks. And most people aren't complicated smart folks. You have *got* to break them of the fear.

You gotta explain that it's an outlet, like racquetball or bridge. You have to explain it's not violent, it's colorful. You want violent? Look at football, look at sports. That's *real actual* violence, not the simulated, stylized, far-from-even-looking-real violence of video games or D&D [Dungeons and Dragons]. And for a real kicker, ask them how many geeks are arrested for violent crimes and misdemeanors when compared to popular athletes.

From a self-described geek mother:

[My] six-year old wonders why he isn't popular on the block, but does not enjoy racing his bike, or playing soccer. (Soccer is becoming fun.) He also wonders why no one else is reading the books he is. The online community did not exist when I was in high school, but geek culture did. Dungeons & Dragons (the original three-booklet set) and science fiction saved me.

How many scared parents have taken the time to introduce their child to the items that kept them sane in high school? How many high school libraries are even allowed to stock Theodore Sturgeon, or all of Robert Heinlein? Before we go to Net culture, we need to face local culture. How many schools enforce a respect-for-all policy, and enforce it fairly? I know that I have a budding geek, and if I can get him sane through the next thirteen years, there will be another decent adult on this planet.

From Armadillo:

I thought I had put this behind me but I obviously haven't. This whole past week has really torn me up inside because 15 years ago, I was one of those kids . . .

I feel like I'm seeing this all through the eyes of a refugee from a war, who by some circumstance is rescued, taken off to a land far from the conflict, far from the danger and death and constant fear and destruction. Years later, after having made some personal peace with the past, if not the people, they hear or see a report that their former hometown or village has been bombed and the people they knew killed and it all comes flooding back.

Why is it that we as geeks, freaks, nerds, dorks, dweebs . . . have to suffer while the clueless, bow-headed, testosterone-poisoned "normal" people are allowed to get away with murder? . . . I wonder just how many outcasts have been driven to suicide because of just one too many tauntings or practical jokes on a particular afternoon?

Why do we murder the spirits of our most gifted and talented young people? . . .

The e-mail was only growing, and I was lagging behind in answering it. More reporters were calling. My friend Jeff said he was going to pull my computer plug out of the wall if I didn't bring this mission to a conclusion.

Jesse agreed. "You've got to stop now, Jon," he said, the concern in his voice surprising. He almost never called me "Jon." He rarely called me anything, but when he had to, "Katz" was the preferred form of address. "If you don't stop, you're going to become their leader instead of a writer writing about them. It will take you over. You can't imagine how much of this is out there. Don't take it all on. Stop now."

When it came to pain, anger, and alienation, Jesse was a leading expert, a hundred times smarter and more experienced than most of the bozos parading across cable talk shows yammering on about the dangers of video games. Why didn't kids like Jesse ever get to go on TV?

Yet scores of them had managed, in the past week, to reach the ears of journalists, to take their firsthand reports to the public. And I didn't want to be a social worker, or the King of the Geeks. I e-mailed Rob at Slashdot and told him I wanted to write a final column. Relieved, he collected all the columns and posted them on Slashdot's archives, where they remain at slashdot.org.

They have worked their way through the labyrinthine links of the Internet and the Web to schools, clubs, websites, chat rooms, and lists, and into the computers of thousands of geeks, for whom Littleton was, on many levels, an all-too-relevant and meaningful experience. It was a piece of the geek story—Jesse's story—but only a piece. I still hear from anguished kids, but far less often; coming in a smaller stream, their stories are both more manageable and less painful.

Yet they affect me, deeply and viscerally; I suspect they always will.

THE PRICE OF BEING DIFFERENT

JOAN McDONALD has been a teacher in a New York State suburban public high school for nearly three decades. "While deeply saddened by the tragedy in Littleton," she wrote Tuesday, "I am appalled at the resulting backlash our students are forced to suffer."

The last thing we need in the twentieth century, she wrote,

is another witch-hunt. But that's what we're getting. McDonald described what hundreds of other teachers, administrators, and students have been reporting all week—an assault on speech, dress, behavior, or values that the media, politicians, and some educators deem uncomfortably different a/k/a geek, nerd, Goth, the usual labels.

In a Gallup poll this week, 82 percent of Americans surveyed said the Internet was at least partly to blame for the Colorado killings. And schools across the country were banning trench coats, backpacks, black clothing, white makeup, Goth music, computer gaming shirts and symbols. They installed hotlines and "concern" boxes for anonymous "tips" about the behavior of nonmainstream students. Kids who talked openly about anger and alienation, or who confessed thoughts of revenge or fantasies of violence against people who'd been tormenting and excluding them, were hauled off to counselors.

Thus the students already at risk, already suffering, have become suspects, linked in various thoughtless ways to mass murder and—consequently—more alienated than before.

"I just came right now from the counselor's office," e-mailed DrgnD. "I scored a thousand. I had on a long coat, was wearing black and loudly told the jerk sitting next to me that I'd do my best to kill him if he ever called me 'a trench-coat freak' again. I am now officially on probation. He is not."

Among the many other consequences of the Columbine High School tragedy: The cost of being different just went up.

Take the Goths, one of the distinct subcultures singled out by the press and linked to the Littleton bloodbath.

One of the most individualistic, interesting, and yes, gloomy subcultures, Goth is a style—of music, dress, state of mind. In general, Goths wear black, hang out on the Net, experiment with androgynous looks, are sometimes drawn to piercings and tattoos with white makeup, and love Bauhaus, Sisters of Mercy, and the Cure. Among their cherished authors are Sartre, Burroughs, Shelley, and Poe. Fascinated with death (a taboo in the media and certainly in schools, along with sex and the open discussion of religion), Goths see it as a part of life.

In general, though, Goths do not hurt people. They brood; they emote; but the idea that they are murderous is a cultural libel.

One of the educational system's pervasive responses to Littleton was to lecture oddballs and geeks about the importance of not slaughtering others. They hardly need such patronizing, offensive lessons about not committing massacres. They're probably one of the least likely cultures in American life to commit homicide; their weapons of choice are electronic flames, not machine guns.

Of the thousands of e-mail messages I got this week (4,000 between Friday and Wednesday is my best guess), not one advocated violence or supported assault, murder, or revenge.

Although many expressed sympathy for the killers as well as the victims in Littleton (unlike, say *Time* magazine, which accompanied cover photos of the killers with the headline THE MONSTERS NEXT DOOR), no one threatened violence, supported it, or approved of it.

But the stories of physical, verbal, emotional, and administrative abuse that came pouring in were stunning, a scandal for an educational system that makes much noise about wholesomeness and safety, but has turned a blind eye for years to the persecution of individualistic and vulnerable students.

The Voices from the Hellmouth series on Slashdot this week demonstrated the power of interactivity and connectivity. Kids passed it around to one another, to parents, friends, teachers, and guidance counselors.

"My seventeen-year-old son handed me a printout of your Littleton article," wrote Bagatti. "No one seems to think that peer abuse is real or damaging. I would like to see any adult report for work and be taunted, humiliated, harassed, and degraded every single day without going stark, raving mad. Human beings are not wired for abuse."

One of the clear messages was that it's time for geeks and nerds and the assorted "others" of the world to assert themselves, to begin defining their long-withheld rights, perhaps using the communicative possibilities of the Net. And to begin the work of restructuring American schools—barely changed in generations despite the ongoing Information Revolution—and their frequently warped structures, procedures, and value systems.

At the very top of the agenda: freedom from abuse, humiliation, and cruelty. Geeks, nerds, and oddballs have the right to attend school in safety. Teachers and administrators have an obligation to make dignity for everybody—not just the popular and the conventional—an urgent educational concern, in the same way they've taken on racism and other forms of bigotry.

Geeks who are harassed and humiliated should report the assaults and, perhaps using the possibilities of the Net, take their complaints farther if they are ignored or further victimized.

Each generation has the right to determine its own culture. Culture isn't just symphony orchestras, movies about dead British royalty, and hard-bound books. For some, culture is now also gaming, websites, chat and messaging systems, TV shows, music, and movies.

No generation has the right to dictate to another what its culture ought to be, or to degrade its choices as stupid and offensive. Yet geek and nerd culture is continuously denounced as isolating, addictive, and, now, even murderous.

Games like Tribe, Unreal, Quake, even the Legend of Zelda and, yes, Doom, can be astoundingly creative, challenging, and imaginative. They are often played in communal and interactive ways. Some people may be uncomfortable with some of their imagery.

But youth culture has frequently been offensive to adults—that's often the point—and culture has always evolved. Adults seem to have no memories of their own youthful lives. Early rock and roll was likened to medieval plagues by the clueless journalists and nervous educators of the time. Now, next to some extreme forms of hip-hop, Chuck Berry seems as dangerous as Beethoven.

Adolescence is a surreal world: Kids who don helmets and practice banging into one another for hours each week are deemed healthy and wholesome, even heroic. Geeks are branded strange and antisocial for building and participating in one of the world's truly revolutionary new cultures—the Internet and the World Wide Web.

Or for being isolated or lacking school spirit. Or for listening to industrial music or wearing odd clothes. But perhaps geek kids are isolated partly because schools don't provide them with any means of connecting.

Inhabitants of a new world with a new culture, geeks often find that the old symbols don't work for them—pep rallies, assemblies, etc. In fact, scholars like Janet Murray of MIT ("Hamlet on the Holodeck") are beginning to explore the ways in which interactivity and representational writing and thinking are changing the very neural systems of the young.

Instead of banning Doom and Quake, schools should be forming Doom and Quake clubs, presided over by teachers who actually know something about the online world (my e-mail indicates that there's at least one frustrated geek on the faculty of most schools). Any school with a football team ought to have a computer gaming, web design, or programming team as well. Geeks ought to see their interests represented in educational settings, to not simply feel pushed to the margins. When these new interests and values are recognized and institutionalized, geek kids may have more status and feel less like aliens in their own schools.

Schools need to provide choices. Educators love to talk empowerment, but few seem to grasp what it means. Geek kids are not, in general, docile and obedient; their subculture is argumentative and outspoken. Online, each person makes his or her own rules, goes where he or she wants to go. Increasingly, it's a difficult transition between freewheeling cyberspace and the oppressive, rule-bound Old Fartism that dominates American education.

"School sucks," e-mailed Jane from Florida. "It's run like a police state, and it's boring and clueless."

Kids raised in interactive environments—with zappers, Nintendos, computers, sophisticated games—often struggle in environments where adults stand for hours droning at them. Their digital world is much more vital, colorful, and engaging than their educational one.

It's the responsibility of schools to create more challenging and interactive environments for its students—a benefit for all younger people who need to learn how to analyze, how to question, how to reach decisions, not just how to take notes and then check the right boxes on the midterm.

And: freedom. Why does the First Amendment end at the school door, when many kids, especially geeks, have spent much of their lives in the freest part of American culture— the Internet? Online, people can speak about anything: dump on God, talk about sex, flame pundits, express themselves politically and rebelliously. In school, no one can.

Geeks, perhaps more accustomed to free expression than their non-wired peers, increasingly and disturbingly refer to schools as "fascistic" environments in which they are censored and oppressed. All kids can't have absolute freedom all the time but many kids, especially older ones raised in the Digital Age, need more than they're getting. Without it, they will become increasingly alienated.

A gaming website like PlanetQuake gets more than 70,000 visitors a day. GameSpy, which helps gamers connect to local games, draws between 60,000 and 80,000. Estimates of online gamers in the United States alone run as high as 15 to 20 million people. The half-baked notion that this activity sparks kids to grab lethal weapons and murder their peers sends a particular kind of message—that the people responsible for educating and protecting kids (politicians, therapists, journalists, educators) have no idea what they are talking about and are posturing in the most ignorant and self-serving ways. It's hard to imagine a more alienating lesson for the young than that.

Finally: Access to popular culture and to the Internet isn't a privilege. It's a right. For many kids, the Net isn't alienation, but its alternative; it's their intellectual, social, cultural, and political wellspring. They need it to learn, to feel safe and

1 7 0 <

connected, and to function economically, socially, and politically in the next century.

Obviously, no right comes without responsibilities—and those should be spelled out both in schools and in families. But access to the Net and to other facets of one's culture ought not be a toy that parents and teachers are willing to dispense to "good" and "normal" boys and girls. For many kids, it's their lifeblood, and it shouldn't be restricted, withdrawn, or used manipulatively except under the most serious circumstances.

It already seems clear from the stories coming out of Colorado that the two young killers were severely disturbed, victims of mental illness about which we know, to date, very little.

But Eric Harris and Dylan Klebold, along with the completely innocent people that they slaughtered, are also victims deserving of compassion. Their illnesses may or may not have been exacerbated by social cruelty and alienation, they may or may not have been affected by access to violent imagery and/or lethal weaponry. We may never be able to answer the *whys* their act provoked. Human minds, for all we're learning about them, sometimes remain mysterious, human acts inexplicable.

Meanwhile, reading all these messages from the Hellmouth this week, I've been overwhelmed by the outpouring of suffering generated by the experience of going to school, and by the brutal price people have paid and are paying for being different. Few people commit violence in schools, but way too many have fantasized about it.

These messages were, in different ways, all saying the same thing. A humane society truly concerned about its children would worry less about oddballs, computer games, and clothing, and more about creating the kind of schools kids would never dream of blowing up.

GEEK VOICES

Jon,

A question—What about us 70+ year olds, are we geeks? Is there an age limit? Your description of geeks seems to fit me in many ways. I'm definitely not a "suit." I guess I can be content with being a contrarian. Keep up the good work, my friend. (If I can ever teach this thing to spell, I might earn this Ph.D. I have.)

—Jordan from Texas

DON'T EXPECT MIRACLES

From: Jon Katz
To: Jesse Dailey

Don't know quite how to interpret this time lag. . . . I have to believe they will get back to you, one way or the other. They don't owe you admittance, but they do owe you an answer. . . .

From: Jesse Dailey
To: Jon Katz

I think I've been pushed to the bottom of the priority totem. I think we just need to make sure they don't forget, but don't expect miracles either. . . .

> > >

BOTH STUBBORN people, Jesse and I had each called the university a half dozen times, but gotten no response. My initial instincts, conjured up by my visit, seemed to have been correct:

Dean O'Neill had graciously made time for me and heard me out, and then common sense had prevailed.

The application was too late. Jesse had not been able to amass a convincing amount of paperwork to show what had to have been a skeptical admissions committee that the university should make room for a geek kid from Idaho with an undistinguished academic record. What were they supposed to tell the record numbers of applicants who had been rejected—the ones with straight As, enthusiastic recommendations, polished essays, and long lists of activities?

The *Rolling Stone* piece had gotten Jesse in the door, no small feat, but not a particularly significant one either. And I had not been persuasive enough on his behalf.

Screw these people, I fumed to my daughter. They sit in their ivy-covered buildings studying dead philosophers while a kid like Jesse gets stuck working for unimaginative shitheads like an indentured servant.

"Easy," she said. "Jesse is great, but he did apply four months late, and a lot of kids have worked hard to get into schools like that." She knew whereof she spoke. Still, I could feel all my old class resentments boiling up.

They could at least have called Jesse back, I groused. He'd killed himself scrambling to fill out all their forms. He'd taken a day off from work to go see Ted O'Neill. He'd been holding his whole life in abeyance pending a decision, and they owed him an answer, at least.

Jesse sounded discouraged, too. More than a month had gone by since his meeting, and he hadn't heard a thing about his status. "I was holding up on looking for another job," he said. "But now, maybe I should start looking around." He sounded fatalistic, talking less and less about college, more about his under-construction new website called Providence.

From my own brief teaching stint, I knew that colleges cleared out by June. Nothing happened; hardly anybody was around to make things happen.

Gradually, we both stopped calling the admissions office.

"I've got to prepare him for it," I told my wife. "It's not going to happen."

From: Jon Katz
To: Jesse Dailey

I can't tell what's going on. I think if there were no chance, he'd just tell you. My guess is that they're just considering it, and it's a bureaucracy that lives by its own rules. If not this place, then another. You're going to college.

Are you discouraged?

From: Jesse Dailey
To: Jon Katz

Slightly . . . yes

We headed into the summer, with the University of Chicago Class of 2003 having gotten their acceptance letters and awaiting news about roommates and registration. There were no more recommendations to collect, essays to write, or people to meet. We were done.

I called one last time to see if I couldn't at least get Ted
O'Neill to send Jesse a polite rejection.

"I'm sorry," said the woman who answered the phone. "He's
going to be away for a week. I'll be happy to take a message."

Uncharacteristically, I didn't have one to leave.

THE LETTER

The University of Chicago
Office of College Admissions

June 11, 1999

Dear Jesse,

I am pleased to inform you that you have been admitted to the University of Chicago, Class of 2003. Congratulations! You should be proud of the accomplishments and promise that led to your selection.

We feel a particularly strong responsibility to admit students who are not only qualified but who are ready to continue the crucial business of educating themselves. You have been selected by our faculty and admissions counselors because you recognize the pleasure—the absolute joy—to be found in the kind of creative labor for which this community of learners and teachers is famous. Our decision was not based on numbers but on your actions and words, a difficult determination to make but one that gives proper honor to the university and to you.

You have the chance to be part of a school with a glorious

history and an exciting present. We look to you to help us grow, to grow with us, and to be part of a tradition that elevates us all.

> Yours truly,
> Theodore O'Neill
> Dean of Admissions

FINITO

From: Jesse Dailey
To: Jon Katz

Looking back, the year seems a bit of a blur, a lot of the way I see the world was changed, and necessarily so. The way I define myself has changed in some ways, but in one major way, it really hasn't. I remember we talked last year before Christmas about David Copperfield, about "having passed through scenes of which [my 'peers'] could have no knowledge" and of "having acquired experiences foreign to my age, appearance and condition." This I think will never change. . . . I will forever be an outsider of some kind.

Behind me is the only reality I have known, the only one I can know, for want of foresight. Last year, I defined myself as a geek, as an "outsider," as antisocial, because of the reality that preceded it. Ahead of me is a life quite different, and yet I don't quite know how different since I haven't lived it yet. It's something I can only imagine. I see now that saying I'm a geek is a form of shorthand for me. Being able to use the word "geek" has helped me a lot to define myself, but not as a mold for me to fit myself into, as a template to help accentuate my differences.

For me, writing this right now, being a geek means being a willing member of a growing community of social discontent, an intelligent community of libertarians, artists, dreamers, and builders. Technology is just the ticket in, the magic is the discontent and imagination, never being satisfied, and being creative about it. Everyone can use a computer, not everyone is a geek.

EPILOGUE

From: Jesse Dailey
To: Jon Katz

<forwarded message from jonkatz>

<Jesse, doesn't the pain and alienation hurt? Doesn't it
<become a part of you?

It does hurt, but in the end it really doesn't matter. It's just
someone else's opinions. . . . It becomes a part of you, it
scars inside, and those scars become a part of you, all people have them, in different places, different degrees, not all
people dwell on them, or nurse them, some of us just keep
going.
   I know it sounds melodramatic, like John Wayne getting
metaphysical, but it's the truth. When faced with conflict,
any system (including the human system) always has two
options, grow and adapt, or die. . . . The more conflict
the more growth. It's a basic concept of evolution and a
key in modern geek faith, in *my* faith. It's basic human in-

stinct to do whatever necessary to grow and adapt and keep on living.

Jesse
"That which doesn't kill us, only makes us stronger."

> > >

JESSE DAILEY had good reason to complain, but he rarely did. He practiced what he preached: To the extent he could manage, he trivialized obstacles, viewing them as building blocks to character and resilience. Technology was the tool that made that possible for him, enabling him and Eric to evade the fate circumstance had chosen for them. Their lives were evidence of the sometimes brutal Darwinian streak in American life.

They had entered high school as classic outcasts, geeks in the traditional sense. But there had been one enormous break—the rise of the Internet in their early adolescence. History, great social and technological change, had swung their way, and they caught a lucky piece of it, grabbed on and rode it out of Idaho toward a different future. Those born a bit earlier or poorer or more technologically inept probably got left behind.

It was Jesse and Eric's geekness that first attracted my attention, that led *Rolling Stone* to publish a story and my publisher to want a book. It has proved a valuable commodity. It was this geekness that inspired Mr. Brown to form a protective high school club, induced companies in Chicago to hire Jesse and Eric practically off the street, got the University of Chicago to admit Jesse and the University of Illinois to consider Eric.

How much did my interest and action affect the direction of

their lives? A fair amount. It was my suggestion that geeks could get work anywhere that started Jesse plotting to leave Idaho, although I didn't know it at the time. I instigated the timing of the move from Richton Park to Lakeview; my friend's check helped make it happen. I talked with Jesse, countless times, when he was discouraged and depressed. I prodded him for months to begin thinking seriously about college.

I back-stopped his application process to the university, made phone calls, reminded him about essays and deadlines and various administrative chores. I went out to the school to argue his case. I'd promised the university that I would stay involved with him through his college years, not just through the publication of this book. And I will.

In the interim, trying to broaden his world and feed his hungry mind, to lure him out of his apartment, I sent books and, once in a while, tickets. I sent him a coffeemaker, a desk lamp so he could read in his room, a baseball cap with a Linux symbol. When I visited, I took him and Eric out for meals that included vegetables.

Small gifts, all of them, to an already independent and enterprising person, but I think they heartened Jesse, gave him some sense of security, that there was a safety net below him. When we first met, I could see that he expected me to vanish at any moment. Over time, he came—cautiously—to see that I wouldn't. His trust in me was touching, my faith in him absolute.

I mention this stuff because I'm obliged to be candid about the support he received, in the interests of honest reporting and a faithful recounting of his journey from Idaho to Chicago. I'm not objective or detached about Jesse or Eric, but I have tried to be straightforward and open about that and about my role in their journey.

They never asked for any of this and resisted almost all of it, except for Jesse's request for help in applying to college. His passion to move forward with his life overcame even his fearsome pride. And he has repaid me in many ways, beyond opening up his life so that I could write a book.

He helped with my online writing, showing me things like gaming, MP3, and the ICQ and Hotline messaging systems—knowledge that was tremendously useful in my Web and Net columns. His insights helped me grasp what was happening in the Hellmouth, decades after I'd fled myself. He reaffirmed my waning belief in the ability of people to change other people's lives for the better, cracked my cynical veneer. I was wrong about the University of Chicago; institutions can do good, can sometimes extend themselves. He even reminded me that lost boys can overcome daunting difficulties and change their destinies, even as I've struggled to change mine.

All along, I was very conscious of the boundaries of appropriate help, something any parent wrestles with daily. I could give Jesse some support, a little material help. But his internal life is his, beyond my reach or influence, as it should be.

Jesse's isolation is something he carries within, not merely something that the world has inflicted. I still haven't understood why someone so personable and articulate has had such a struggle to forge connections with others.

I've been largely unsuccessful at guiding him toward a more balanced life, but we both know that this is something he has to do for himself—or not. A social life, he once wrote me, "is not something you turn on and off like a switch, it's not a process that can be initiated at the behest of the processor. It cannot be treated as a maneuver, or dealt with in terms of tactics, and strategies." In this and other ways, Jesse is wiser than your standard twenty year old.

"To tell the truth, despite my best efforts, none of my girlfriends (both of 'em, lol [laughing out loud]), could quite figure out how to settle with someone as . . . as . . . well, as Geeky as me," he wrote me last summer. "One was intelligent, very free, but never stable, she just ended up being quite the young alcoholic and I couldn't deal with that, I tried and so did she, but I just couldn't stand her drinking. Oh well . . . I've turned the search for The One over to the muses, and I'll let the worlds decide." A particularly revealing, even hopeful message: Jesse hadn't given up on the idea of love, he was simply putting it aside for a while.

WHEN I told friends about these two kids, and about what had happened with the University of Chicago, the first question they asked was, "What about Eric?" It was much on my mind.

Jesse and I talked constantly about Eric, who was happy for his pal, but also clearly unnerved and depressed at the prospect of losing the one person in the world he completely trusted.

Jesse had been prodding Eric for two years to be more outgoing, communicative, and optimistic; he hadn't gotten far. Sometimes Eric felt good about work, sometimes grimly pessimistic. His oft-expressed dream of advancing into the higher levels of research science—at NASA, Caltech, or MIT—came up less frequently now, his bleak funk descended more often. If life in an office tower—"I swear, it was just like *Dilbert,*" he told me—had energized Jesse into wanting something more, igniting his perpetual restlessness, it seemed to drain Eric.

For the first time since we'd met, he didn't always answer my e-mail promptly. But he did stay in touch, sending occasional messages like these:

From: Eric P. Twilegar
To: Jon Katz

Hello Jon,
    Things have slowed down a bit here at work. Probably because everyone is heading off for the four-day weekend. Good news abounds for Jesse, can't say much is really happening in my life. I'm not sure quite what to think about the future. I definitely know I'm torn. On one hand is a life of science and little money, and the other a life of boring development for quite a bit more $.
    Either way I have to get some schooling. I don't think I'm feeling comfortable about going to school in the spring, but maybe I should anyway. DePaul has kinda popped up again too. I have to say timidly that I'm a little scared. Maybe I am just a wanderer.

From: Jon Katz
To: Eric P. Twilegar

Eric, I'm not sure what that means. Nobody can force you to go to school, of course, it's your choice. Like Jesse, you are sure smart enough to do it if you want to. And I'll help you in any way that I can. Have things been satisfying at work?

From: Eric P. Twilegar
To: Jon Katz

. . . not much of anything. I got a lot done on my program Friday and Saturday, most of the framework is done, now I just have to write a good user interface.

I think I'm going to start running after work to cool down a little, and to get rid of the pouch I'm forming. :) The next 6 months is just going to be hell. I might be able to get a contract or something. But I still have to pay the rest of my bonus back. Plus being a contractor is no fun. All day I wish I was at home coding . . . this tech support crap is getting out of hand. I'm stagnating and there is no way out.

From: Jon Katz
To: Eric P. Twilegar

Eric, I disagree. There is often a way out, especially at your age, and as you proved last year. But do you have to define your life so narrowly in terms of programming?

From: Eric P. Twilegar
To: Jon Katz

it's the only thing I got.

From: Eric P. Twilegar
To: Jon Katz

I always have tried [to get interested in other things], but have failed miserably with all of them. I don't know if you can understand, but going out and trying to do what other "normal" people do is so uncomfortable for me that it's not any fun. I really try to go out to things and enjoy myself, but all they do is make me feel bad about myself.

From: Jon Katz
To: Eric P. Twilegar

Eric, you sound pretty down. Can I help?

From: Eric P. Twilegar
To: Jon Katz

only I can help myself

His messages almost always ended on the same note of despair and resignation.

Jesse had changed enormously since we'd first met in Idaho, and in the months to come would change still more. His generous, outgoing side would emerge; he would even start to look different, less pale and hunched. Eric hadn't changed much. Profoundly guarded in many ways, Jesse was inherently optimistic: Faced with a problem or dilemma, his conclusion was usually that he could find a way to solve or survive it. Eric's, increasingly, was that he couldn't.

For all that they shared, Jesse had developed a passionate, profoundly upbeat view of technology as a means to alter fate and circumstance. Eric also loved science, but saw fate and circumstance as inalterable. Their differences took on a poignant note, now that their parting seemed inevitable.

Earlier in the spring, Eric had wanted very badly to go to

188 < JON KATZ

school and was planning to apply to Illinois for the fall of 2000. He had all the forms and had started filling them out. But then he balked. He hated school, he wrote. He wasn't sure.

In early July, he e-mailed me he was not going to apply, and would probably stay on in the Lakeview apartment, saving his money for a career change in his mid twenties.

From: Eric P. Twilegar
To: Jon Katz

. . . one thing you have to remember about me is, I hate school. I love learning, but not in the medium our education system does things. Going to lots of classes, jamming shit-loads of info down your throat and testing you on it and then grading you on how well you did it. . . . Perhaps some day school will be less of a capitalist nest.

From: Eric P. Twilegar
To: Jon Katz

Hey Jon,
   Thought I'd end the silence. Things are going pretty good. . . .
   The next few months are definitely going to be weird for me. Jesse is such a huge chunk of my life. It will be nice to have the place to myself, but very lonely. But I see a good side to it. At the moment I have very little motivation. It has always been a flaw of mine. To settle into situations like this. So far I have been lucky enough to have big change whip me out of the holes. It seems like fate has helped me out again. Now I will have to try the dating game out, and will definitely have to meet someone outside of work.

Hopefully life will continue to be interesting at least. If not, oh well.

Don't worry, I'll be fine.

I worked to keep in contact, and to remind him that life was no more fixed at twenty than it had been at nineteen.

Meanwhile, Jesse and I were embroiled in the endless details of his getting ready to be a student again. His last contact with a doctor had been at a phys ed check-up in high school, so he needed immunizations. He'd have to figure out where to go during school vacations. "I guess it will be like being a foreign student," he said.

There were a million financial aid forms to fill out, which involved contacting his parents and digging out tax records. Neither of his parents were in a position to help out financially, and he still didn't know how much the university might provide. I would be struggling to pay my own kid's tuition; I couldn't tackle Jesse's. Since he—and I—had been so clear about his lack of money, we both hoped the university financial aid office would come through.

When it came to handling bureaucracies, though, Jesse was a master; I knew once he got into the school, he'd figure out ways to stay there.

His big fears came when he pondered the differences between his academic background and the experiences of his new colleagues. "I'm trying to go online to figure out how to do a college paper," he told me. "I've never done anything like that."

I explained that the university understood that "nontraditional" students would need help. He'd have to ask, but help would be there. And I pointed out that if he devoted half the time he spent online—which would amount to roughly twenty hours a week—to studying, he'd succeed and still hone his geek skills.

My hunch was that Jesse would become indispensable, helping to maintain the university's computer systems, providing tech support to half the school, maybe even getting Dean O'Neill online to track down websites featuring his beloved Enlightenment philosophers.

In the interim, more preparation.

We went over the list of things he'd need, from notebooks to a bathrobe. Jesse wondered if he really needed a dresser; couldn't he just keep his clothes in a plastic bag, as usual? I was firm about the dresser.

Many of these discussions took place in Eric's presence, and Jesse and I were both conscious that it was probably painful. But Eric told me a dozen times how profoundly appreciative he was just to be where he was. He had a secure job that paid well and offered prospects for advancement. That, he reminded me, was a hell of an improvement over Caldwell.

And, said Jesse, he'd give Eric his queen-sized bed. What had happened to Eric's water bed? I wondered. The one he'd hauled from Idaho? Eric had never gotten around to filling it up in Chicago, Jesse said, so he'd been sleeping on the beanbag chair.

Beyond the pragmatic concerns of furniture, computers, and medical forms, Jesse and I talked, too, about more amorphous issues. Like identity—he'd long had a penchant for defining himself by what he wasn't: a preppie, a suit, a yuppie. But what *was* he? A geek, but that was only part of any person.

"I dunno," Jesse said. "I guess I'm going to find out. Sort of the point, huh?"

Leaving Idaho had freed him of the need to taunt Mormons; nobody in the big city cared what his religious views were. I thought going to the University of Chicago would probably dilute at least some of his hard-core geekness, since he was, in a way, joining a larger tribe of brainy geeks, nerds, and outsiders. "I'm withholding judgment," was all he would say about that.

Jesse never dared permit himself to think he'd have fun. Or that there might really be a community he could join. This, more than any other aspiration, had eluded him for so long and caused so much hurt that he simply did not allow himself to consider it.

He did say he was postponing construction of his website, Providence, until he got to the university. He thought it fitting that it coincide with starting college.

"Plus I bet you'd love to piggyback on one of the university's servers and put the site up at their expense, with their bandwidth and memory," I observed. He conceded that the thought had crossed his mind.

Apart from the logistics, however, he was excited about the symbolism of launching Providence in September. He sent me a logo, the third he'd designed, and attached a definition:

"Providence, *n*. 1. The act of providing or preparing for future use; a making ready, a preparation for things to come."

But nobody's life is simple or unambiguous. People in the mainstream, non-geek culture are right to be worried about Jesse and his generation. Fond as I am of many of them, geeks are often profoundly alienated from many of the elemental responsibilities, institutions, and traditions of American life.

They have acquired enormous power, but don't frequently take moral responsibility for what they do, for what they have. They tend to believe in a world in which people take responsibility for themselves—and only themselves. They don't see themselves as part of the political fabric of American life. They watch events like the Monica Lewinsky drama and increasingly turn away from the lunacy of mainstream culture to the rich, free, and diverse world of the Net and the Web.

Jesse's generation is lost to the press, to the newspapers and newsmagazines and broadcasts that, until recently, were the nation's common, universal information providers, agenda setters, and value shapers. Geeks recoil from journalism's relentlessly phobic, shallow, and hysterical portrayals of their culture; they simply disconnect. The best these institutions can hope for is to hang on until the next generation comes up. Maybe, by that time, they can do better.

Jesse's notion of "propaganda shit," a term used widely on the Net, is disturbingly broad: journalism, politics, much of education. There is no politician in Washington, or almost anywhere, whom people in the geek culture respect or pay much attention to, or who respects and pays much attention to them. It's sometimes hard to believe that people like Jesse, as cynical as they are skilled, will ever reconnect to the political system that governs this country.

The geek nation is profoundly contemptuous of the education it's gotten, and resentful of its treatment by most schools. Free to say and do what they please on the Net, geeks bristle at schools' restrictive, noncreative environments. The cultural values of mainstream institutions—sports, clothes, popularity—are alien to them, while their own distinct beliefs and skills often go unrewarded and unacknowledged.

Deeply suspicious of businesses as well, they see large corporations as greedy, arrogant, and inhuman institutions, which makes it easy to pilfer from them at will.

The only institutions that can draw solace from the Geek Rise are the entertainment companies that dominate pop culture. Geeks' passion for music and certain movies and TV shows is undiluted. Next to the Net, pop culture is their ideology and their common language. It may be one of the few reliable ways left for mainstream society to reach an elite that's too skeptical and wary to domesticate, but too smart and creative to write off.

OVER THE past ten months, I'd developed too much affection for Jesse to keep up the pretense of a purely journalistic relationship, something I unapologetically acknowledge.

Jesse's told me more than once that he doesn't know how to categorize our relationship. He already has two parents, and I have a kid.

Yet we both understood that I had slipped into a quasi-parental role, especially when it came to applying to college.

Did it make him uncomfortable, I asked him one night, that I had sometimes usurped his parents' place? Strange, he said, not uncomfortable.

Despite his feelings for his parents, he said, he knew they would "be out of place dealing with the University of Chicago. Any discomfort I have about you being here instead would be a lot higher if they were here."

Like most kids his age, he was awkward about even discussing this. The closest he could come to describing what we are to one another, the one time I pressed the matter, was that I'd become a kind of "uncle, maybe."

"I'd describe our relationship as a friendship," I told him when we subsequently revisited the question. "We are good friends to each other. You are a very good friend to me." Of all the descriptions, I think that was the one we both liked best.

But when you write a book like this, I've warned him, first and foremost you have an obligation to be honest, to play fair with the reader, to share everything that shaped the story. So I have to do that here. Sorry, Jesse.

As is probably quite obvious, I have come to love this kid. It's a strange, unlikely evolution from a project that began as a straightforward journalistic inquiry.

I love his pluck, his humor, his bravery, his passion for technology, and, perhaps most of all, his bedrock integrity. Jesse is a pioneer. He's building a new culture, and in the best geek tradition, even if he has no clear idea how, hopes to use his knowledge for the greater good of humanity.

His life gives testament to the idea that the outcasts are coming inside. After long and bitter persecution, they are taking their rightful place at the center of society—valuable, in touch with one another, even appreciated. The fact that a fabled university wants Jesse as a student is a startling metaphor for this new reality.

Jesse's story embodies all the promise, shortcomings, and contradictions of the revolution he and his geek army are busily engineering. Many of these issues will play out for him at the University of Chicago:

In a world so absorbing, tempting and engaging, how can school compete? What will become of the traditional benchmarks of civilization—books, music, culture, politics? The Internet offers kids like Jesse unprecedented opportunity. But does it also make it tougher—or easier?—to build the elements of what we consider a stable life: family, friendship, balance, some sense of spirituality, a willingness to engage in the sometimes unpleasant tasks of life in a common society?

The rise of Jesse and his comrades ought to serve as a wake-up call (as I suspect it did for Dean O'Neill) for the institutions responsible for guiding our society—journalism, politics, education. Most have done poorly by these kids. They've also done a generally wretched job of preparing us for the staggering changes technology will bring.

A generation ago, Jesse and Eric would probably have been the kids who ran the projector during school assemblies—the only ones in the school who knew how to splice the film when it broke and get the movie rolling again. Since that wasn't a terribly important function in the scheme of things, the projector kids languished at the bottom of the social pecking order. Their successors—Jesse, Eric, and their fellow members of the Geek Club—now know something much more important.

And because they do, they are no longer ignored. Often, in fact, they are feared and resented for knocking the pecking order to hell. They are often the only people who really know how the world works.

Is this good or bad? Certain techno-utopians are heralding a brilliant future while certain Luddites are sounding the alarm that civilization itself is being eroded. There's a case to be made either way. The great technology writer Samuel Florman calls this the tragedy of technology, reflecting the best human impulse to improve and tinker with the world, and the just as powerful human tendency to screw things up.

Jesse is part of a revolution that will change many of our conventional understandings about the world and how it works. As one scientist said, the Internet is like the discovery of fire. It makes possible developments we haven't begun to imagine. Things will be lost as well as gained. The historians will have to sort it out.

For me, a perpetual outsider looking in, a restless man on the periphery of mainstream institutions, a geek in his soul if not in his computing skills, my heart is with Jesse and the free, raucous, engaging new civilization he is helping to invent.

Much as I love studying and writing about the species, I was born too early to be a full-fledged member. But I'm lucky to see it. And thrilled that this part of the story ends this way:

I arrived at my cabin in upstate New York one warm summer

evening in June. The crickets were practically shaking the ground with their noise. I'd come to write this book, though I wasn't sure how I'd end it. I threw open the windows of the musty house, and saw the answering machine blinking. One message.

I played it back. It was Jesse, speaking in a voice tinged with a kind of excitement I'd never heard before, that he'd never permitted himself. He was breathless, childlike, speaking twice as fast as normal—"Hey Jon, this is Jesse. I just got a letter from the University of Chicago today, and it's a letter of acceptance. I got the fat envelope! You give me a call when you get in. 'Bye."

My first reaction was disbelief, followed by rich, inexpressible joy. I called Jesse up and we screamed "Awesome!" and "Cool!" at one another for five solid minutes. Then I had to get off the phone, or I would have gotten squishy.

"Does this make you a preppie now?" I jeered before hanging up.

"No," Jesse shot back, King of the Last Word, as ever, "just an infiltrator of the preppie regime."

A million fireflies were winking in the meadow as I carried the answering machine out onto the porch and plugged it in. Across the valley, the mountains stood out against the dimming sky.

I played the message several times, sending Jesse's words rolling down the meadow, across the valley, out into the world, even though there was nobody within miles who'd hear it.

I was glad he wasn't there. He disliked any show of emotion, and I would have had to feign restraint. Instead my eyes welled up. For Jesse, and, a bit, for me. And also for the geeks, nerds, oddballs, misfits, the alienated, the different, the non-normal— all the names given over decades and centuries to the Others— for whom it was too late.

The geek had ascended.

AFTERWORD

IN SEPTEMBER of 1999, I flew out to Chicago to accompany Jesse to his freshman registration. Eric came along to help tote Jesse's belongings, which consisted of computer equipment, a few haphazardly packed cardboard boxes, and several crammed duffel bags.

I didn't think either Jesse or I would make it through the day. The registration process was overwhelming and chaotic. Fittingly, the computers broke down, and the lines for student IDs and course selection grew blocks long in the late-summer heat. When Eric left to head home, Jesse—still gaunt and pale in his geeky sneakers, polyester short-sleeved shirt, and ancient oversized glasses—looked as panicky and uncomfortable as I'd ever seen a human being look. He was surrounded by harried, shouting administrators and highly educated, well-groomed yuppies, the type he'd always perceived as his natural enemies. Somehow, he had voluntarily stepped into his own worst nightmare.

He had little money, a minimal wardrobe, no bed linens or furniture, not even toothpaste or an alarm clock. Standing there in the crowd, he was conspicuous, nothing like the high-powered boomers' children, who had been bred from birth for places like the University of Chicago, and who were now forming a ceremonial procession down the middle of the campus.

It was an emotional scene. The class of 2003 marched with parents, friends, and other family members down a street lined with Gothic stone buildings and hundred-year-old trees. At the end of the street, the procession divided and the students went one way, their parents the other, serenaded by mournful bagpipers. Hundreds of people were in tears, parents and kids breaking down and sobbing in more or less equal numbers.

I had just gone through a similar drama the week before when my wife and I dropped our daughter off at college. But in one sense, this was harder. Deep down I feared I was leaving Jesse alone to face a difficult future in an alien world.

After all, he hadn't been in school for two years, and when he was, he'd paid little attention to his studies. He'd never written a scholarly paper in his life, or learned how to use a library. Now he was about to begin classes at an institution known worldwide for its demanding academic traditions, surrounded by kids who were used to pulling all-night study sessions and getting good grades.

The next few months were indeed brutally difficult, for both of us. Jesse got slammed by one crisis and challenge after another. I spent days on the phone with university administrators and bureaucrats, exhorting them to watch over him, pay attention to him, help him sort through the bureaucratic, academic, and personal tasks for which he was so unprepared. Jesse had an almost toxic relationship with bureaucracies. He seemed to bring out the worst in them, and vice versa. Although he never talked of dropping out, Jesse was often profoundly discouraged, at times bewildered, humiliated, overwhelmed.

We talked on the phone three or four times a week. I visited him on several occasions, as I had promised the dean I would, and as I wanted to, to help him feel settled and to slog through the innumerable crises that erupted: vaccinations, financial aid, tact in dealing with professors and teaching assistants, a part-time job, a daunting workload, social concerns. I was soon on a first-name basis with a wide variety of counselors and advisers, most of whom put up with my fussing and hovering with good humor and patience. Once they were aware of Jesse's situation, they wanted to help. The problem was, he never asked, at least not at first. It was a rough time for Jesse, rougher perhaps than for anybody else, but I knew, since I was one of the few people who knew where Jesse had come from.

THAT MARCH, *Geeks* was published amid much noise online and -off, and I flew once more to Chicago, for a book signing at the university and some media appearances. It had been a couple of months since my last trip, and just a few weeks since the latest crisis—involving tardy financial aid forms—that had driven Jesse nearly mad with frustration.

On a brilliant spring day, my cab pulled up to the funky and ancient dorm, Breckenridge Hall, that had been Jesse's home since September. I stepped out and began walking toward the bookstore. Up ahead, to the north of the beautiful, spacious

Quad that anchors the university, I spotted some kids horsing around. One was riding piggyback on a buddy's shoulders, laughing, his right arm hanging on to a beautiful young woman who was looking up at him, smiling and holding his hand.

It didn't even occur to me that this might be Jesse until he turned my way, spotted me, and waved. He jumped off his friend's back, came loping over, and threw his arms around me. I was overwhelmed at the sight of this happy, healthy young man; everything about him, from his haircut to his posture, was different.

It was almost disorienting to try to reconcile this person with the Jesse I had first encountered—depressed, discouraged, un-dernourished, hunched, barely able to look me in the eye. A kid who had renounced the chance of social acceptance for good, and fled his own town and home life. He was now so at ease, so happy in his crowd of pals, that my eyes welled up. I stood watching, shaking my head.

Although he'd struggled at first to catch up with his mostly better-prepared and -equipped peers, Jesse had coped with college life much better than either of us could have imagined. He'd joined up with a small band of mostly working-class kids. And an intense and lovely young woman from New England who had stormed into his room from time to time to share freshman crises and trade information had become a friend, and the friendship, Jesse explained to me, had become a "thing." He wasn't sure himself exactly how it happened, but he was clearly delighted that it had. His friend wasn't particularly geeky, nor much interested in computers, though he'd quickly got her hooked on some games.

The love and acceptance that had eluded him for years in Idaho seemed to almost fall into his lap in this very different environment. When I visited now, I had two college students, not one, to take out to dinner.

SO JESSE has done well, to answer the question I get asked via readers' e-mail at least a dozen times a day. He not only survived the transition to one of the most demanding educational institutions in the country, he did so with flying colors and, ultimately, good grades.

I was—and am—enormously proud of him. I don't think I can fully articulate how daunting the struggles were that he encountered—paperwork, money problems, organizational and family issues, brutal academic challenges, new and strange social realities—or how resolutely he faced them down one by one. Nor is that a story Jesse wants me to tell in much detail.

But as the year developed, I also noticed that he identified himself less and less as a "geek," even though his love of computing was undiminished and he still spent hours on a computer nearly every night. In fact, by the middle of the year 2000, it was difficult even to say what a geek was. Everyone was online, from grandmas to CEOs, and the world's passion for technology was stronger than ever.

At the University of Chicago, there was less need for Jesse to be The Other, no real role for a Mormon-taunter. He was surrounded by a community of discontents, oddballs, free thinkers, and free spirits. In a sea of intellectual misfits and geeks of different natures, he could drop much—though by no means all—of the wariness and many of the defense mechanisms that had enabled him to survive in Idaho. He was beginning to see that he was free to be pretty much whatever he wanted to be—and that people would relish his company and contributions on account of it.

For me, a middle-aged man whose daughter had gone off to college at the same time as Jesse, our relationship was a gift. At a time when I was braced to confront an empty nest, I found I had twice as many kids to guide and watch over as the year before. And despite the geographic and cultural distances, Jesse had a new family of sorts that he cared deeply about.

Eric has also done well, although his story is, as always, more ambivalent. He initially decided against college, rented an apartment in Chicago's Lakeview section, and took a new job as a database administrator for an online travel service, a highly geek-friendly environment. Jesse took considerable care to introduce his new friends to Eric, and Eric's apartment became a valued off-campus gathering spot and haven for Jesse and his pals, who trekked over on the train every week. Jesse's friends were moved by Eric's increasing openness, sweetness, and generosity; anything of his was theirs. His friendship with Jesse not only continued but deepened.

Eric also made friends of his own, hosted LAN (computer networking and gaming) parties, dated, and dealt directly and successfully with some of the depression that had been plaguing him his whole life. Even if he wasn't thrilled with every aspect of his life, he was pleased to be out of Idaho. He loved Chicago.

Predictably, however, work occasionally began to feel too

routine. Just as Jesse had, Eric began to sense a ceiling that would limit his future if he didn't have some sort of higher education. In May, he announced that he had decided to take my advice after all, and would apply to the University of Illinois. I thought it was a great move. He told me he wanted the title "Doctor" in front of his name one day. He's smart enough to make that happen. I hope he does.

THE PUBLICATION of *Geeks* proved to be a profoundly happy and meaningful experience. I got to travel all over the country—in two cities, Jesse came along—talking about technology with hundreds of kids and parents. I also got to see how challenging and painful life still is in schools for the brainy, obsessive, individualistic, and alienated.

At first, on tour, I was overprotective of Jesse, warning publicists, producers, and talk-show hosts that he would rarely be available to talk, and only under very controlled circumstances. After all, the only media experience he'd ever had was yakking with me. But in Chicago, he asked if he could accompany me on a few stops. Reluctantly, I agreed.

I felt pretty stupid that same evening when Jesse virtually took over a two-hour radio talk show, fielding questions and offering opinions with the ease and confidence of a pro in pancake makeup. I could barely get a word in edgewise; after a few minutes, the callers forgot about me and began directing their questions right to Jesse. Curiously enough, it was only in listening to Jesse talk about *Geeks* that I truly began to understand what the book was really about.

Geeks was never primarily a book about computers, the Net, technology, or even geeks. It was—is—a very human, almost classically American story about two plucky, brainy, rebellious outsider kids from a little godforsaken town who headed to the big city to make their fortunes. Technology fits into the story like this: Without the Net, Jesse would never have found me, or I him. He probably wouldn't have gone as far, as fast, as he ended up going. He surely would have bettered his life—he's way too gifted to have remained a small-town computer repair technician—but in many ways, the Net pulled him through. It gave him a community and an identity, an education when he needed it most. It then assumed less centrality in his life as he settled down to the long-delayed business of figuring out who he was in the world, and what he really wanted to do.

One of the most perceptive reporters I encountered on the tour, Margot Adler of National Public Radio, saw instantly what *Geeks* was about at heart and made me, and thousands of listeners, see it as well. When all was said and done, she said, it was about mentoring, about the willingness of one person to enter the life of another, someone temporarily needy, and offer a hand.

That was both wise and true. In response to one of Jesse's many declarations of thanks and appreciation for the process that led him to Chicago, I e-mailed him that no thanks were necessary. My only wish was that one day, should he come across another Jesse, he would reach out and try to pull him along. He said that he would.

We live in a detached, cynical world. But you can make a difference in people's lives. You can affect outcomes. You can reach even people who are culturally, politically, and socially very different from you and, with encouragement and support, help them build a better life and get places they want to go.

THE NATURE of my relationship with Jesse has continued to evolve. We are comfortable together, affectionate in the way of people who have been through a lot together and have come to trust each other, not a common experience for either of us. We still argue on and off about the future of Microsoft, whether or not the Web will be "corporatized," whether nanotechnology will truly change the world. But we also fantasize about the possibilities for Jesse. Happy discussions, exciting choices: What might he do, what should his major be? What kind of work will he seek, and where might he live? How can I get him to take a creative writing course, with hopes that some professor might spot his other great gift?

For me this is, of course, bittersweet. As any middle-aged parent (or mentor) learns, if you do your job well, you'll become obsolete, still important but only sporadically necessary. I can see this happening already. Jesse, now completely at home at the University of Chicago, a place where he knew from the first he always belonged, has less need of me. I need to monitor him less. Our affection for each other has grown, but his life is finally pulling him along, as it should, toward the friends, peers, and challenges his extraordinary mind and admirable character have always deserved.

So along with immense pride and satisfaction, loss is just around the corner, life rambling on in its familiar way. Jesse's future, whatever form it takes, will not much involve a fifty-year-old writer halfway across the country. And I'll miss that. He knows that I will be there for him, even as I know something he doesn't: He won't need me much, or for much longer.

Early on in our friendship, Jesse offered one of his characteristically wise observations. When you do something for other people, He said, you are often doing something for yourself. True. And writing *Geeks* is one of the best things I ever did for me.

ABOUT THE AUTHOR

JON KATZ is the author of *Running to the Mountain* and *Virtuous Reality*, as well as six novels. He has written for *Wired, New York, GQ,* Hotwired, and *The New York Times* and was twice nominated for the National Magazine Award for articles in *Rolling Stone*. He writes on the Web for Slashdot.org and Free!, the Freedom Forum's website. He lives in Montclair, New Jersey, with his wife, Paula Span. He can be e-mailed at jonkatz@ slashdot.org. He can also be reached via ICQ: 18891303 and AIM ID: Quasimodem47.